Nordic Traces in Israel

Orna Keren-Carmel

Nordic Traces in Israel

Orna Keren-Carmel
European Forum
Hebrew University of Jerusalem
Jerusalem, Israel

ISBN 978-3-031-75286-5   ISBN 978-3-031-75287-2 (eBook)
https://doi.org/10.1007/978-3-031-75287-2

© The Editor(s) (if applicable) and The Author(s), under exclusive license to Springer Nature Switzerland AG 2024

This work is subject to copyright. All rights are solely and exclusively licensed by the Publisher, whether the whole or part of the material is concerned, specifically the rights of reprinting, reuse of illustrations, recitation, broadcasting, reproduction on microfilms or in any other physical way, and transmission or information storage and retrieval, electronic adaptation, computer software, or by similar or dissimilar methodology now known or hereafter developed.
The use of general descriptive names, registered names, trademarks, service marks, etc. in this publication does not imply, even in the absence of a specific statement, that such names are exempt from the relevant protective laws and regulations and therefore free for general use.
The publisher, the authors and the editors are safe to assume that the advice and information in this book are believed to be true and accurate at the date of publication. Neither the publisher nor the authors or the editors give a warranty, expressed or implied, with respect to the material contained herein or for any errors or omissions that may have been made. The publisher remains neutral with regard to jurisdictional claims in published maps and institutional affiliations.

This Palgrave Macmillan imprint is published by the registered company Springer Nature Switzerland AG
The registered company address is: Gewerbestrasse 11, 6330 Cham, Switzerland

If disposing of this product, please recycle the paper.

Contents

1 **Book Introduction** 1
  The Nordic Path 3
  The Israeli Path 6
  The Beginning of Nordic-Israeli Relations 8
  Israel and the Nordic Countries: Special Relations 9
  Beyond Politics 10
  A Future Look on Nordic-Israeli Relations in the Past 14

2 **The Grey Truth: The Danish Rescue in Israeli Holocaust Memory** 17
  The Rescue of Danish Jews in Israeli Holocaust Memory 19
  Israeli Historiography of the Rescue 21
  Between the Particular and the Universal 24
  Layers of Commemoration 25
  Rescue and Politics 26

3 **Ben Gurion, the Nordic Countries and the Neutral Bloc** 29
  Nordic Cooperation 32
  Aid Policy to Developing Countries 37
  Israel-the Nordic Countries-Africa 40

4 **Nordic Wooden Huts and Israeli Public Housing** 51
  Housing Shortage 53
  The Nordic Wooden Hut 56
  Nordic Wooden Huts as Public Buildings 59
  From Temporary Housing Solution to Nostalgic Asset 61

5 "Adolescence is a serious problem of life": N. F. S
  Grundtvig, Martin Buber and Adult Education in Israel 69
  *The Long Path to the Establishment of the School
  for Educators of the People* 71
  The School for Educators of the People 73
  Grundtvigian Inspiration 76
  Teacher-Student Relations 77
  Adult Education and National Identity 79
  Adult Education as Response to Extreme Situations 81
  Implicit and Explicit Inspiration 82

6 Common Values, Different Interests: Early
  Israeli-Swedish Cooperation on Development Aid
  to Africa 89
  Mount Carmel Training Center 91
  Early Years of Development Aid 92
  Swedish-Israeli Cooperation on MCTC 94
  International Cooperation 98
  Bilateral vs. Multilateral Aid 99
  Social Democratic Development Aid 101
  Circulation of Knowledge 103
  The End of Swedish-Israeli Cooperation on MCTC 105

7 Mission: The North. Concluding Travel Notes
  from Scandinavia 115
  Leni Yahil 116
  David Ben Gurion 119
  Shmuel Yosef Agnon 123
  Alex Carmel - A. Trempai 126

Index 131

CHAPTER 1

Book Introduction

Abstract The introductory chapter reflects the structure of the book, according to which every chapter presents one case study that became a milestone in Nordic-Israeli developing relations over the years. Together, all case studies offer a new overall analysis of their relationship, proving the common denominators underlying these countries, such as similar socialdemocratic values and strong professional unions. In addition, the case studies map Israel geographically in accordance with diverse Nordic-Israeli initiatives, enabling a graphic interpretation of their ties.

Keywords Nordic path · Israeli path · Nordic -Israeli connections · special relations · social democratic

Since 1948, when Israel was established, its relations with the Nordic countries, Sweden, Denmark, Norway, Finland, and Iceland have had ups and downs. From a bird's eye view, it is customary to characterize the relations forged between them in the first two decades i.e. the 1950s and 1960s as benevolent and close, the 1970s as a period of crisis, the next three decades as consistently deteriorating, and since the second decade of the 2000s as a period of stabilization, albeit occasionally marked by crises. During the past few years, and particularly following the Russian-Ukrainian war that broke out on February 2022 as well as the war in the

© The Author(s), under exclusive license to Springer Nature Switzerland AG 2024
O. Keren-Carmel, *Nordic Traces in Israel*,
https://doi.org/10.1007/978-3-031-75287-2_1

Middle East that broke out on October 7, 2023, relations with Denmark, Finland, and Sweden have clearly strengthened. The recent decision of Finland and Sweden to abandon their long-standing neutral stance and join NATO has also paved the way for closer ties to Israel, in light of the new emerging geopolitical situation.

In general, Nordic-Israeli historic relations revolved (and in some aspects still revolve today) around three main orbits, which were often intertwined: Holocaust commemoration, social democratic common vision and policies, and the Israeli-Arab/Palestinian conflict. Nevertheless, the numerous studies that have been published on their relations over the years mostly focused on their different approaches to the Israeli-Arab/Palestinian conflict.[1] This perspective, as interesting as it may be, neglected all other areas of their relations, and failed to explain what made them especially loyal allies for quite a few decades.

This book focuses on the first stages of the relationship that developed between the countries, the "honeymoon period," by providing a comprehensive historical analysis that traces the process of building the complex yet fascinating ties between them. Apparently, precisely the points of contact between them, which were based on their similar approach in the 1950s and 1960s, became the seeds for the crisis that developed later.

Academic research on the beginning of relations between Israel and the Nordic countries hardly exist. While research on the Second World War in Northern Europe has aroused interest over the years, and many aspects of the Holocaust in this region have received substantial research attention in the last three decades, the relations that developed between the Nordic countries and Israel after its establishment—and the threads that connect these two events—are noted in Israeli and international research only in relation to specific events, even if significant: the votes of the Nordic countries in the UN regarding the establishment of the Israeli state, the involvement of Nordic UN officials in the attempts to solve the Israeli-Arab/Palestinian conflict, the murder of the Swedish mediator Count Folke Bernadotte in 1948, and Norway's support for the Israeli nuclear program. The purpose of this book is to provide these events with a general context by filling the historical space between them.

The book focuses on Israel's relations with Sweden, Denmark, and Norway (referred together as the Scandinavian states), and less with Finland and Iceland, since the latter's relations with Israel at the time were sympathetic but quite limited. Finland was busy with the complex relationship with its neighbor, the Soviet Union, and Iceland focused on internal affairs more than on its foreign relations. However, since the book deals among others with the tightening of Nordic cooperation in the early years of the Cold War, it occasionally mentions both Iceland and Finland.

Even though this book represents the first comprehensive study of early Nordic-Israeli relations, it is by no means complete. This new and still unexplored historical field needs further and more detailed research. I have mainly, but not exclusively, used primary sources from Israeli Archives for this study, which thus emphasize the Israeli perspective on the developing relations. A deeper understanding of the bilateral relations between each Nordic country and Israel, as well as their national considerations toward Israel, is still needed. The book is based for the most part on documents from the Israeli Foreign Ministry, government discussions and policy documents originating from the Israel State Archives and the Central Zionist Archives (some of the files that were used are still closed to the public), which mainly illuminate the political and (Labor) movement connections forged between the countries. To complete the research, documents from Yad Vashem Archives, Lavon Institute for Labor Research, Yad Tabenkin Archives, MCTC (Mount Carmel Training Center) Archives, Hebrew University Archives, Swedish National Archives, and Swedish International Development Cooperation Agency Archives (SIDA) were used.

THE NORDIC PATH

Often, the year 1945 is presented as the year zero in Europe, a year in which the patterns of the past were completely erased and a new era began. In the Nordic countries, in particular, this representation is not only inconsistent with reality, but in many ways, it is the opposite of what actually happened. In the policies of the Nordic countries in the post-war period, sequences can be identified more than far-reaching changes. One of the well-known examples is the continuation of the forced castration policy (in Sweden for example until 1975), which was aimed at citizens who, in terms of the state, were unfit to reproduce, in contrast to the vast majority of countries who discontinued this policy at the end of the Second World War, after it was severely contaminated by Nazi Germany's racial Eugenic vision.

In the Nordic countries, the Second World War was integrated into two long-term and complex processes that began in the 1930s and ended about a decade after the war. The first process was the establishment of the Nordic comprehensive welfare state. The welfare legislation in the Nordic countries, which recognized the duty of the state to act first and foremost for the benefit of its citizens, began already at the end of the nineteenth century, but was established with the social democratic governments in the 1930s. In Denmark, for example, the authorities established the right of Danish Jews to compensation for the losses they suffered as a result of the Second World War immediately upon their return to the country, on the basis of the principles embodied in the 1934 disability pension law for victims of the conscripted forces.[2] In Sweden, too, the state's increased involvement in the lives of the refugees who arrived there (inter alia in the areas of food, housing, education, employment, health, and leisure) led to the adaptation and expansion of the welfare legislation that already existed, also to refugees and immigrants.[3] Thus, although the Second World War in the Nordic countries was an event that brought about a deep social change, the change was integrated within the local populations according to the principles of the universal welfare policy that was shaped before the war broke out.

The second significant process that the Nordic countries went through, in which the Second World War was integrated, was the design of the Third Way. In 1936, the American journalist Marquis Childs published a book titled *The Middle Way*, in which he praised Sweden's successful navigation between (American) capitalism and (Soviet) communism in the socio-economic field. The political extremism that developed in other European countries throughout the 1930s which led, among other things, to the outbreak of the Second World War, justified for the Nordic countries the moderate approach they chose. The choice of the Middle/Third Way, along with the attempt to maintain neutrality (Sweden was more successful in this, Denmark and Norway less so), was a guideline in the conduct of Sweden, Denmark, and Norway from the 1930s and throughout the war, and even more after its end and throughout the Cold War.

During the Cold War, the Nordic countries strengthened their regional cooperation. Although the plan for a Nordic defense union and the plan for a Nordic economic union were not realized, in part because of the pressure exerted by the Soviet Union on Finland not to join and in part because of the accession of Denmark to the European Union (1973), other significant collaborations did succeed: in 1952 the Nordic Council was established, which was composed of members of parliament of the five Nordic countries; in 1954, the Nordic Labor Agreement was signed which opened the employment market equally to all citizens of the Nordic countries; and in 1971, the Nordic Council of Ministers was established, which was made up of committees of ministers from the five countries to coordinate a uniform policy in a variety of fields.

In the late 1940s, the Nordic countries began to deepen their involvement in the international arena and even take a position in the ongoing Arab–Israeli conflict in the Middle East. At first, they tended to adhere to the British position on the conflict, since in those years Great Britain was their main ally, but a few years later they began to formulate a more independent position. Their involvement was manifested in support for Israel's establishment, for its security policy in the context of the various conflicts that emerged in the 1950s and in votes in the United Nations in Israel's favor. The high presence of Nordic observers and mediators in the Middle East—whose professional position was often different from that of the politicians in their countries of origin—also contributed to the Nordic involvement in the region.[4] For example, the difference in the reactions of the Nordic countries to the assassination in Israel of the first UN mediator on Palestine, the Swedish Count Folke Bernadotte, reflected not only the gap that existed at the time in the Nordic countries between the attitudes of the general public and the attitudes of officials regarding the young Israeli state, but also the difficulty of the Nordic countries, due to the differences between them, to formulate a uniform Nordic reaction.

Over the years, the Nordic countries have invested a lot of efforts in developing a similar, albeit not uniform, foreign policy, which testified to their uniqueness as a distinct geographical-political entity: small and neutral moral powers that strive to resolve international conflicts, to promote human rights throughout the world, to establish close regional cooperation, to support a liberal immigration policy and to provide international development aid. These elements in the Nordic foreign policy were combined with its unique domestic policy, i.e., a comprehensive welfare policy, the pursuit of gender equality, broad political compromises, and an emphasis on adult education. The combination of this exceptional domestic and foreign policies in the Nordic countries led to the creation of the famous Nordic model. In the last decades this model, which was only retrospectively formed into a comprehensive theory, serves as an example of proper policy, as evidenced by the consistent positioning of the five Nordic countries every year at the top of the index tables published by the Organization for Economic Cooperation and Development (OECD).

The Israeli Path

Israel's first decade, 1948–1958, transformed the country into a sovereign state. The main issues that the state's leadership was struggling with at the time included the establishment and development of a strong army to preserve its unstable borders; absorption of a large number of Jewish immigrants from European countries as well as Jewish communities in Muslim countries—in just three years, between 1948 and 1951, Israel's Jewish population doubled from 650,000 to 1,322,000—and providing them with housing, work, health care, and education; promotion of new settlements all over the country: from the Negev in the south through Jerusalem to Galilee in the north; shaping of international recognition for the Israeli State; search for available energy sources; development of research and technology as a basis for modernization and industrialization processes; and finally, strengthening the Labor Movement, as a theoretical as well as practical tool for the fulfillment of the aforementioned challenges.

First Prime Minister David Ben Gurion was an experienced statesman, both pragmatic and visionary. It did not take him long to understand that dealing with these many internal challenges requires massive external help from friendly countries with a positive attitude toward Israel. This is why Israeli historian Uri Bialer called his comprehensive book on Israeli early foreign relations *Israeli foreign policy: a people shall not dwell alone* (Bloomington, Indiana University Press, 2020). Ben Gurion made a bold choice that emphasized the desirable as well as necessary element, in his opinion, in the development of independent foreign relations of the State of Israel: he avoided frontal confrontations with the Soviet Union while building a relationship based on trust with the Americans. He objected to the attempts to divide the Middle East into zones of influence. Israel's policy in these years—from both an international and a national point of view—was as a corollary often described as neutral within the inter-bloc struggle.

The second decade to Israel's existence, the years 1958–1968, was a decade of both continuity and great transformations. A trend of consolidation was evident in many areas: demographically, the population continued to grow (although not at the same steep rate of the first decade); the national product per capita doubled throughout the decade; the cultivated agricultural areas increased by about 500%[5]; the industrial sector expanded into new areas such as chemical factories, textile factories, security factories and food factories; in 1958, the cornerstone was laid for a nuclear reactor; the port of Eilat was opened to international trade in 1965 and the maritime port of Ashdod was inaugurated in 1966; finally, infrastructures were established and developed in areas such as transportation, primary and higher education, and in the health system. The communication infrastructure was also expanded: the first telephone conversation in kibbutz Sde Boker in the Negev took place on February 2, 1958, between the Minister of Posts Yosef Burg and Prime Minister David Ben Gurion who lived there in his Finnish wooden hut.

At the same time, the second decade also witnessed significant changes in Israeli politics and society. In 1963, Ben Gurion retired from his authoritative state's leadership, after 15 years as head of the Zionist movement and as prime minister (except for the years 1953–55). It was also the decade of the awakening of two new sectors in Israeli society: the Mizrahi—the new immigrants who arrived from Islamic countries in the previous decade, and the Arabs—who began to organize themselves as a new political and social force separated from the Jewish establishment.

Israel's foreign policy also expanded in this decade, even though the first and most important goal in its international priorities continued to be ensuring the existence and security of the country. Accordingly, the countries in which Israel invested the most efforts were the ones that could provide it with weapons for defense. In 1948 it was Czechoslovakia, in the 1950s France and Great Britain, and in the 1960s West Germany and then the United States. At the same time, Israel cultivated intensive relations with the African sub-Saharan countries, among other things with the aim of expanding the number of countries that recognize and support it in various votes in the United Nations. The relationship with them was intended to curb dangerous organizations against Israel in the General Assembly and the Security Council of the United Nations, as well as to promote strategic security interests.[6]

The second decade ended with the 1967 war, which led to far-reaching changes in Israel's foreign relations. The quick and surprising Israeli victory, the changes to the borders of Israel, and the significant rapprochement with the United States—both in terms of arms supply and economically, changed within a few years the paradigms that had dominated until then among Israeli decision-makers. A decisive change, if also one of the least known, was the effect of the war on Israel's relations with the Nordic countries. This change became a pivotal factor in the crisis in their relations that occurred during the next decade, 1968–1978. But this is a topic for a separate in-depth study.

THE BEGINNING OF NORDIC-ISRAELI RELATIONS

The early connections between the Jews in Palestine and the Nordic countries can be traced back to the first decades of the twentieth century. But it was the Second World War that created new and unique connections between them. Already during the war, the Nordic populations received considerable gratitude from the Yishuv (Pre-Israel's Jewish population) for their support of their Jewish communities against Nazi persecution. However, it was only during the 1950s and 1960s that an overwhelmingly positive and heroic representation of the Nordic countries' conduct toward their persecuted Jewish minorities took shape in the Israeli culture of memory, stemming from the close relationship that forged between the countries in these two decades. That is, contrary to the common claim that the benevolent relations between the countries developed because of the Nordic countries' helpful conduct toward their Jewish communities during the Second World War, in fact the process was the opposite: it was the constructive political and professional relations between Israel and the Nordic countries during the 1950s and 1960s that led to the retrospectively shaping of an extraordinary benevolent interpretation of the conduct of these countries during the Holocaust.

After the war, the Nordic countries, led by Denmark, Sweden, and Norway, sought to increase their involvement in the international arena by becoming a small but effective political bloc. The path they chose, with Sweden at the head, was to adopt the image of moral superpowers, that is, small countries that have a solid moral standing and strive tirelessly to preserve human rights within and outside their countries. The events of the Holocaust in Northern Europe were integrated into this image with hindsight. The Norwegian Resistance enjoyed the image of fighting the Nazis fiercely, as well as saving as much of the country's Jewish citizens as possible, against all odds; Sweden focused on the rescue operations of Raoul Wallenberg and Folke Bernadotte, in addition to the generous rehabilitation of refugees who came to it during and after the war; Denmark became a "ray of light in the darkness of the Holocaust," a nation with strong democratic-humanist roots that succeeded to save almost all its Jewish co-citizens; and Finland became famous for the inexistence of the "Jewish Problem" within its borders. Thus, all Scandinavian countries and Finland were awarded, as a group, a benevolent international representation as rescuers—a representation that is woven to this day in their authoritative image in the field of international humanitarian aid.

The second chapter of the book thus explores the formation in Israel of this positive representation of Holocaust events in Denmark. The story of the rescue of thousands of Danish Jews in October 1943, during which they were smuggled by boats to neighboring Sweden, has become one of the most stable myths in the Israeli Holocaust memory. However, from the 1940s to the present day, there have been significant changes in the memorial culture in Israel, and these have reshaped in turn the attitude toward the Danish people, its underground fighters, and the survivors. The chapter examines the broad and changing historical context of the rescue story against the background of the shaping of Israeli national ethos, and reveals how the myth formed around the rescue not only helped to bridge the gap between the past and the present and between the horrors of the Holocaust and the morality of the rescuers, but also contributed to shaping the national identity of the young Israeli society.

ISRAEL AND THE NORDIC COUNTRIES: SPECIAL RELATIONS

During the 1950s, the formal and professional links between Israel and the Nordic countries tightened. The Labor movements in Israel and in the Nordic countries conducted mutual training of workers, consultations and exchanges of delegations, and sought similar solutions to the problems the welfare states were facing at the time. As a result of the professional ties, warm relations were often created between the labor circles, especially between senior officials in the Histadrut (Israel's General Federation of Labor) and senior officials in the trade unions of the Nordic countries.

The third chapter thus deals with the emergence of the special relationship between the Nordic countries and Israel in the second half of the 1950s, which was largely based on their social democratic bonds. In those years, similar to the Nordic countries, Israel also shaped its path in the field of foreign relations. The fact that Israel was not invited to participate in the Bandung Conference, held in Indonesia in 1955 for all African and Asian countries, exacerbated the feeling of isolation that prevailed in Israel and highlighted the need to find international allies. This chapter unravels the efforts of Prime Minister David Ben Gurion to have Israel join the Nordic neutral bloc, and thus cooperate on political-security levels with the Nordic countries, in an attempt to stay unaligned and to avoid having to choose a side in the polar rivalry of the Cold War.

Ben Gurion's initiative to fulfill his vision was designed to get closer to the Nordic countries by cooperating on providing aid to developing countries in Africa. Like other developed countries in the late 1950s, the governments of Sweden, Norway, and Denmark also began to take an interest in the de-colonialized countries of Africa and Asia that had recently gained independence, and wondered how they could be integrated into the aid efforts for them. At first, they tended to channel their activities through the aid institutions of the United Nations, alongside the establishment of joint Nordic projects such as a teaching hospital in South Korea in 1958 and a Nordic project in Tanzania in 1963. But over time, the Nordic countries decided to tighten their cooperation, not only to enable solutions on a larger scale to the many problems from which the developing countries suffered, but also to provide them with a practical example of how cooperation between countries can benefit each of them individually and all of them together.

The many attempts by senior officials in the Histadrut and the Israeli government (mainly Foreign Minister Golda Meir and Prime Minister Ben Gurion) to convince the Nordic governments to cooperate on development aid were unsuccessful. The northern countries were indeed afraid of the reaction of the Arab world to the proposed tightening of relations with Israel, but this was not the main reason for their refusal. At the end of the day, even though they did not always see eye to eye, the Nordic countries preferred to cooperate with each other in the field of international aid rather than with other countries. The Nordic connection, to Israel's disappointment, turned out to be a Gordian knot.

Beyond Politics

Since the time of the Vikings, and especially since the mid-nineteenth century, the Holy Land has been a source of attraction for Nordic pilgrims, primarily from Sweden. With the establishment of the State of Israel, the Lutheran connection created with Jerusalem led the Swedes not only to support the transformation of the city into an international entity in order to preserve its status, but also to initiate proposals on the matter within the framework of the United Nations. After 1948, some of the religious institutions established by the Nordic countries before Israel was founded were allowed to continue their activities, including Tabor House in Jerusalem—founded by Konrad Schick and serves until today as the Swedish Theological Institute—and the Scandinavian Seamen's Church in Haifa.

However, the close relationship that developed between the Nordic countries and Israel during the 1950s led to the establishment of further ties in a wide variety of new fields. From the early 1950s, young men and women from the Nordic countries began to arrive in Israel, at first little by little and then in an ever-increasing flow, to experience kibbutz life—the utopian socialist experiment—to travel and to get to know its residents. For the most part, they returned to their countries of origin highly impressed by the young Israeli country. In the strategic field, Norway agreed in 1959 to sell Israel heavy water that enabled the construction of a nuclear reactor. Municipally wise, Petah Tikva in Israel and Norrköping in Sweden were declared twin cities and later the former also became a twin city of Odense in southern Denmark and of Trondheim in central Norway. Also in the touristic field, after considerable difficulties SAS opened an airline to Israel and tourists from all five north European countries could visit destinations that were considered particularly exotic until then (one of SAS's commercials to promote tourism to Israel presented the throwing of a microfilm of Israeli *Herut* newspaper over the North Pole). In the field of culture, as well, extensive connections were formed between the countries. The Israeli Bezalel Academy of Art conducted student exchanges with art schools throughout the Nordic countries. Israeli painters presented exhibitions in the Nordic countries and their colleagues exhibited in Israel. Furthermore, on the occasion of the 10th anniversary of the State of Israel in 1958, a tour of performances by the dance group *Inbal* and the singer Shoshana Damari was held in all Nordic capitals.

Nevertheless, it was mainly the literature that compelled the residents of Israel toward the Nordic countries. For example, the books of the Norwegian writer Knut Hamsun, and especially the reference in his book *Growth of the Soil* (1917) to the pioneer settlement spirit of the first and second Aliyah (the waves of Jewish immigration to the Land of Israel), were a resounding success in Israel, and his influence was clearly evident on the later writings of Shmuel Yosef Agnon and Isaac Bashevis Singer. Knut Hamsun's sympathetic attitude toward Nazi Germany was hardly ever mentioned in Israel. The series of children's books by the Swedish writer Astrid Lindgren and the photographer Anna Rivkin-Brick, which describe the daily life of various children around the world, were translated into Hebrew in the 1950s by Leah Goldberg, and enjoyed widespread circulation and many editions along the years, including very recently.

The following chapters of the book, chapters four, five and six, offer three examples of the close and constructive relations that evolved between Israel and the Nordic countries, which testify to their similar social democratic worldview. Chapter three presents the considerable Nordic influence on Israeli public housing in the 1950s. Following the need for rapid housing solutions, resulting from the steep demographical rise after the establishment of the Israeli state, thousands of imported Nordic wooden huts became part of the Israeli landscape. These wooden huts were not only an important contribution to the building of Israel, but are still nostalgically commemorated in our own days. Chapter four explores the fascinating connections between the ideas of the Danish educator N.F.S Grundtvig and the Israeli philosopher Martin Buber, as reflected in the establishment of "Beit-HaMidrash Lemorei Am" (School for Educators of the People) in Jerusalem in 1949. In many ways, Grundtvig's mid-nineteenth century vision on adult education, translated and updated by Buber, was realized a century later in Israel. Chapter five describes the Mount Carmel International Training Center, a joint Swedish-Israeli initiative that was established in 1961 in Haifa in order both to offer African women practical training in various fields and to train Nordic experts before they were sent to their aid missions in Africa. The termination of this joint center, maybe not surprisingly, coincided with the deep crisis in Israeli-Swedish relations in the late 1970s.

Despite the above, or perhaps because of it, in the 1950s the seeds of the crisis in Israel's relations with the Nordic countries, which occurred more than two decades later, also sprouted. Two factors emerged from the study that could explain it. First, between the 1950s and the 1970s, a generational change took place. The relationships between leading socialists in Israel and in the Nordic countries, which were developed in the 1930s, were manifested in the political and movement echelons in the 1950s and 1960s, when these people established themselves in key positions in the social democratic governments and trade unions in all six countries. In the late 1960s, this generation of leaders began to change and as a corollary the considerable effects of the close personal relationships forged between the leaders dissipated and disappeared.

Second, Israel and the Nordic countries chose different paths. Already in the 1950s it is possible to recognize, alongside the great similarity, the differences that began to take shape between the countries. The international status enjoyed by the Nordic countries as a neutral bloc of moral superpowers, advocating the resolution of regional conflicts by adhering to the decisions of international institutions, stood in contrast to Israel's developing policy, which in many areas preferred national considerations over compliance with international agreements and focused on conflict management over comprehensive political solutions. This difference could also be explained by the ostensibly similar but essentially different international status they adopted during the Cold War's early years: as neutral states, Sweden and Finland were subject to the rules of international law governing relations between belligerent and non-belligerent states, while Israel defined itself as non-aligned and thus was not subject to such laws. However, there were also other substantial differences in the foreign policies of the countries. While the Nordic countries put a greater emphasis from the 1970s and onwards on the Third World, on resistance to American participation in the Vietnam War, on national liberation movements and on mediation, Israel at the same time has clearly abandoned its non-alignment policy and became a close ally of the United States. These shifts have significantly contributed to the process of distancing in later decades.

The conclusion chapter of the book is presented through the accountings of four Israelis who for various reasons have visited the Nordic countries during the 1950s and 1960s: Prime Minister David Ben Gurion, Nobel Prize winner author Shmuel Yosef Agnon, Historian (and wife of the contemporary Israeli Ambassador to Sweden) Leni Yahil, and the adventurous journalist Alex Carmel. The writings of these four persons, following their visits, describe feelings of closeness and brotherhood as well as feelings of misunderstanding and sometimes even of disappointment that characterized the relations between Nordics and Israelis in those years. Furthermore, their accountings refer to the vast majority of the subjects that the book deals with—the shaping of memory around the Second World War and the Holocaust in the Nordic countries, the complex political relations, the close ties between the trade unions, the international consequences of the Suez war in 1956, the shared social democratic vision, the different attitudes toward the UN and its international agreements, etc. Therefore, as well as being a testimony of primary sources of that time, the last chapter also embodies its conclusion.

A Future Look on Nordic-Israeli Relations in the Past

This book contributes to research on the relations between Israel and the Nordic countries in three different but complementary areas. First, it presents a new, lesser-known angle of Israeli foreign policy in the first two decades of its existence. The studies that have been conducted to date on Israel's international policies in those years mainly discuss the complex relations it had with the great powers, the Soviet Union, the United States, France, Great Britain, and West Germany. The place of the Nordic countries, which at the time were loyal and significant allies of Israel, is absent. It presents, on the one hand, Israel's attempts to avoid as much as possible involvement in international conflicts originating from the Cold War, and on the other hand, its rapprochement with peripheral countries such as the Nordic countries, at the expense of supporting one of the superpowers. In addition, the study testifies to the importance of the developing persuasion system of the State of Israel (Hasbara) as an essential part of its foreign policy.

Second, the book sheds light on the formation of the external and internal borders of the Nordic bloc. During the 1950s, the Nordic countries adopted a Third Way that embodied neutrality in foreign policy and a universal welfare system in internal affairs. The external point of view provided by the study—Israel as a geographically distant country but close in terms of governance—testifies not only to the unification process of the Nordic countries, but also to the need to set limits for the cooperation of each Nordic country, alone and as part of the Nordic Council, with other countries. Additionally, it examines the durability of the Nordic countries' definition as one geographical-political-cultural entity whose policies are similar, through the question of whether they conducted their relations with Israel as one body, or whether, in each case, national considerations prevailed.

Finally, while most of the historical research on welfare states tends to focus on the development of their unique domestic policies, this study intends to explain the process of shaping their foreign policies. Did the social democratic values, which in the 1950s were common to Israel and the Nordic countries, lead to increased cooperation between them, or did they rather accentuate the disagreements between them? The political relations that developed between the ruling parties of Norway, Denmark, Sweden, Iceland, Finland, and Israel, as well as the relations between their labor movements, were based to a large extent on the professional relations between their trade unions and other social institutions, and the personal relations between senior officials that were created as a result. The research thus reveals the importance of one of the special elements of the welfare state—strong labor movements—as a stable basis for cooperation in a variety of fields and consequently a significant tool for improving interstate relations.

At the end of the day, this book reveals the historic differences, and surprisingly also the similarities, between the Israeli and the Nordic perspectives in fields such as welfare, security, adult education, housing and development aid, during the first few decades after Israel's establishment. These revelations might lead the readers to re-examine the understanding of the welfare state's unique relations with its citizens, as well as the manifold possibilities for bilateral cooperation between different welfare states.

Notes

1. Recent, well-researched examples are Nir Levitan, *Scandinavian Diplomacy and the Israeli-Palestinian Conflict* (Routledge, 2023); Jacob Eriksson, *Small State Mediation in International Conflicts: Diplomacy and Negotiation in Israel-Palestine* (IB Tauris, 2015); and Daniel Schatz, "Sweden's Middle Policy at a Crossroads", in *Israel Journal of Foreign Affairs* (2018).
2. Bak Sofie Lene, "Repatriation and Restitution of Holocaust Victims in Post-War Denmark", *Jewish Studies in the Nordic Countries Today*. Scripta Instituti Donneriani Aboensis 27 (2016), pp. 134–152.
3. Byström Mikael, "When the State Stepped into the Arena: The Swedish Welfare State, Refugees and Immigrants 1930s–50s", *Journal of Contemporary History* 49, no. 3 (2014), pp. 599–621.
4. A partial list includes the members of the committee for the implementation of the distribution plan, the Dane Per Federspiel and the Swede Paul Mohn; the first mediator to the resolution of the conflict in the Middle East, the Swede Folke Bernadotte; the first UN Secretary General, the Norwegian Trygve Lie; the second UN Secretary General, the Swede Dag Hammarskjöld; and the Danish observer, Vagn Bennike.

5. H. Yablonka & T. Tsameret (eds.), *The Second Decade: 1958–1968* (Yad Yitzhak Ben-Zvi, 2000), pp. 7–8.
6. Uri Bialer, *Israeli Foreign Policy: A People Shall Not Dwell Alone* (Indiana University Press, 2020), pp. 231–232

CHAPTER 2

The Grey Truth: The Danish Rescue in Israeli Holocaust Memory

Abstract The rescue of thousands of Danish Jews in October 1943 is one of the most persistent myths in the memory of the Holocaust in Israel, together with the fishing boat that became the symbol of that rescue, during which the Jews were smuggled to neutral Sweden. However, from the 1940s until today, there have been considerable changes in the Holocaust memory in Israel, and these reshaped the attitude toward the Danish people, the Resistance fighters, and the survivors themselves. This chapter examines how the myth that was formed around the rescue not only helped to bridge the gap between the past and the present, between the horrors of the Holocaust and the morality of the rescuers, but also contributed to the shaping of the Israeli national identity.

Keywords Denmark · Rescue · Second World War · Holocaust · Memory · Survivors

---

This chapter is based on my article published in Hebrew in *Zmanim*, 141 (2019), pp. 64–75. I would like to thank the editors of the journal for the permission to publish it here in English.

© The Author(s), under exclusive license to Springer Nature Switzerland AG 2024
O. Keren-Carmel, *Nordic Traces in Israel*,
https://doi.org/10.1007/978-3-031-75287-2_2

On April 9, 1940 Nazi Germany occupied Denmark, and Hitler offered the Danish government a tempting proposal: in exchange for acknowledging German superiority in Europe—meaning surrendering in advance—and conducting Denmark's foreign affairs, Denmark would maintain its sovereignty and manage its internal affairs on its own. It only took a few hours for the Danish government and King Christian X to agree to the offer, hoping thus to preserve Denmark's economy, exports, and businesses, while minimizing the harm to its citizens and their possession. So began a political and economic cooperation of Denmark with the German occupation force.

Until the end of the war in May 1945, a complex yet close relationship was forged between the two countries, which directly affected the fate of Danish Jews. The option of the Danish government to negotiate with the Germans, together with the reluctance of the two states to violate the utilitarian relationship that had formed, led the Germans at the moment of truth to avoid a frontal confrontation over the "Jewish problem" in Denmark. Consequently, the property of the Danish Jews was never expropriated, they did not lose their jobs, they were not forced to move to Ghettos, and they were not required to wear the yellow Star of David. The fact that Danish Jews were not marked as a separate group devoid of any rights created a real possibility for a large-scale rescue in the autumn of 1943. The Jews still had friends, neighbors, colleagues, and acquaintances that were willing to help them. Furthermore, at the time of their escape, the Jews still had sufficient economic resources to enable their hiding places, and, later on, their flight to Sweden. Finally, the announcement by the Swedish government in early October 1943 that it would accept with open arms all Jewish refugees from Denmark, cannot be underestimated.[1]

On August 29, 1943 a state of emergency was declared in Denmark. The government was dissolved and the German plenipotentiary Werner Best decided to take advantage of the opportunity and "clean" Denmark of its Jews. On the night of October 1, 1943, the planned date of deportation, Gestapo units went out, together with Danish volunteers, to arrest all the Jews, but because the planned date was leaked a few days before, only a little less than 500 Jews were arrested that night and in the following days. All the rest, about 7200 Jews and another 700 non-Jewish family members, found refuge in the homes of friends, acquaintances and even complete strangers, or fled to the forests or to summer houses near the beaches. During the following three weeks, Danish Jews crossed in fishing boats to the shores of neutral Sweden, among others with the help of the Danish Resistance. The Germans, who knew about their escape, turned a blind eye. Over 99% of the Danish Jews survived the Holocaust.

The Rescue of Danish Jews in Israeli Holocaust Memory

In an article in *Haaretz* newspaper dated October 30, 2013, Knesset (Israeli parliament) member Michael Melchior described the great weight given during the Eichmann trial, which took place in Jerusalem in 1961, to the testimony of his uncle, David Werner Melchior, who was part of the Danish rescue operation:

> Apparently, my uncle's testimony, regarding the saving of the Danish Jews, did not add anything to the indictment against Eichmann, but Judge Bach [retired Supreme Court Judge Gabriel Bach, one of the prosecutors during the trial - O.K.C] made it clear to me that there was a significant message in it [...] The masses who followed closely the horrifying testimonies could have concluded that when choosing between good and evil, human nature will always choose evil. My uncle, who shared in his testimony the story of the rescue of the Danish Jews, helped the prosecution by proving that there are not only individuals but also entire nations, who, when faced with difficult choices, decide to choose the good even at the risk of their lives.[2]

The Eichmann trial contributed significantly to the internalization of Israeli society that the Danish rescue was extraordinary, exemplifying the exception that proves the rule. It demonstrated the loneliness of the Jewish people in the Diaspora and the indifference of the rest of the nations of the world to its fate, and thus reaffirmed the need for an independent Jewish state. At the same time, the trial provided the opportunity to place the Danish rescuers in a moral-human context, according to which their actions expressed the proper character for Israeli citizens to adopt, and were thus intended to contribute to the shaping of the contemporary Israeli national character.

Nevertheless, when Mordechai Shenhabi, one of the chief planners of the Yad Vashem institution (Israel's official memorial to the victims of the Holocaust), suggested to Benjamin Slor, a senior member of the Jewish community in Denmark, to honor the Danes for saving their country's

Jews and to award them the title of "Righteous among the Nations," the latter reacted with mixed feelings. His reply in English, on June 28, 1947 was interwoven with handwritten Hebrew expressions:

> It is a right and beautiful thought to start the list over the [Righteous among the nations] with the former Danish king, Christian X: a more worthiness name to start with cannot be found. I also think that the greater part of the splendid, deep in their hearts democratical, Danish people with the royal house in the head, will appreciate it very much; but if this will be the case also with regard to the greater part of the Danish Jewry, I am not so sure [marked by the Hebrew expression: "and enough a word to the wise..." – O.K.C]. Apart from above mentioned it may not be forgotten that in all here, we only have about 7000 souls, and that the majority of the Danish Jews have still not recovered in full from the difficulties caused economically by the war.[3]

This short passage raises two main questions: first, what did Slor mean by the expression "and enough a word to the wise..."? Why didn't the surviving Danish Jews want to cherish their Danish saviors, all the more so in 1947, after the extent of the extermination in the rest of Europe became fully known? Second, the mention of the precarious economic situation of the Danish Jewish citizens contradicts the common image that was formed after the rescue, according to which the citizens and authorities in Denmark fiercely protected not only the lives of the Jews but also their property.

The testimonies of the survivors from Denmark who immigrated to Palestine and later Israel after the war greatly add to these bewilderments. In most of them, sometimes explicitly and sometimes implicitly, there is a tone that undermines the prevailing and positive image that has formed in Israel in regard to the rescue operation, according to which the democratic and human Danish people came out as one to defend their persecuted Jewish minority. For example, Dov Gerstensang, who at the age of 6, in 1939, crossed the border from Germany to Denmark illegally with his family, said in his testimony to Yad Vashem in 2003 that the Danish authorities were evil and no better than the German ones, that for many months they tried to deport his family from Denmark and that their lives were saved only thanks to the Germans' refusal to accept them back.[4] Also, the survivor Yehuda Kuper, a member of the "Hechalutz" who came to Denmark in 1939, described in his memoir *That's how it was* from 2003 an incident that happened to him and his wife during their escape: during the voyage from Denmark to Sweden, in the middle of the sea, the fisherman declared that there were too many refugees on the boat and transferred both to another boat. After that, Yehuda learned that the fisherman demanded an additional amount of money from the refugees who remained on his boat, and that those who could not pay were required to hand over their jewelry and clothes.[5]

It appears that at least in the first years after the rescue, the attitude toward it was complex: along the glorification of the conduct of the Danes, other voices were also heard, who tried to present it in a broader historical context. How, then, did the rescue later become a "ray of light in the darkness of the Holocaust" and an unprecedented example of large-scale rescue by the local population? The answer to this question is intertwined with the developments that took place in the Holocaust collective memory in Israel.

The formation of the myth on the rescue of the Danish Jews—a process that began as early as 1942, about a year before the rescue even took place, and continued until the end of the 1960s—occurred at a central intersection in Israeli society: on the one hand, there was the need to remember the events of the Holocaust, the recent and terrible past, and to commemorate them, and on the other hand, the people needed this moral-valued "national ethos" in order to educate in its light younger generations. Therefore, the myth shaped around the rescue not only helped to bridge the gap between the past and the present and between the horrors of the Holocaust and the morality of the rescuers, but also contributed to shaping the national identity of Israeli society, its past and its vision for the future. Between these two significant roles of the myth— the construction of memory and the shaping of identity—there existed, and still exists, a self-feeding relationship: identity shaped the object of memory, and memory provided the identity with content.

Israeli Historiography of the Rescue

Leni Yahil, Israeli historian and the pioneering researcher on the rescue of Danish Jewry, emphasized in the introduction to her 1966 book *The Rescue of Danish Jewry—Test of a Democracy* her Zionist point of view in analyzing the events of the Holocaust in general and that of the rescue in Denmark in particular.[6] This point of view, along with the comprehensive and thorough research she conducted on the rescue, led Yahil to one main conclusion: although the rescue of the Danish Jews is an example of positive and moral human behavior, the future of the Jewish nation is only guaranteed in its own, independent state. The fact that the Danes chose to save the Jews of their country—and even succeeded—proves that all the other nations refused to act in this way. If they were as resolutely opposed as the Danes were to the deportation of the Jews, the murderous plan of Nazi Germany would not have come to fruition on the same scale. Despite being based, therefore, on a positive historical event, the meaning of the lesson derived is rather pessimistic: there is no hope for the integration of the Jews in countries other than Israel.

One of the prominent consequences of Yahil's representation of the rescue in Denmark is the disconnection of the rescue event from the wider context of the Second World War: it became at the same time both connected and not connected to the historical events that took place in the years 1939–1945 in Denmark. Like the Holocaust in general, the rescue event was also recounted as inside a bubble, solely from a Jewish perspective on the interrelationships between foreigners and Jews throughout the generations. This component of the Holocaust discourse did not succeed in internalizing the rescue event except as a counter-example: the Danish population was the only one of all European populations that refused to participate in the extermination of its Jews, and for that they deserved special recognition. The special conditions and circumstances that enabled the rescue in Denmark, both from the Danish and the German side, did not correspond to this one-dimensional view, and therefore they were not part of the story of the rescue that was shaped.

Another important consequence is the concept of resistance. After the defeat of Nazi Germany, during the reconstruction of the European continent, the issue of resistance to Nazism was central in all the countries that were freed from the occupation. In Denmark, a country that continued to work in close cooperation with Nazi Germany until the end of 1944, the story of the resistance gained a unique importance, and became an essential part of Danish national identity after the war. The image of the successful rescue of the Jews with the participation of the entire nation—from the king to the last of the fishermen—became the culmination of the story of the resistance.

In Israel too, the Danish rescue story became a representative model of collective heroism during the Holocaust, but from a slightly different angle. The rescue operation testified to the heroism of the Danish people: a united entity, headed by the king, with a resistance movement that refused to surrender to the Nazi plans and staunchly defended its democratic-human values. This representation suited the somewhat simplistic way in which the Holocaust was presented in Israel during the 1950s: the exceptional rescue of Danish Jews was often contrasted with the central phenomenon of non-resistance and passive behavior toward the occupying German power on the part of local populations. In addition, at that time, the survivors from Denmark who emigrated to Israel rarely spoke publicly about their experiences from the time of the war because most of them did not see themselves as having experienced the horrors of the Holocaust first hand, and also because the public concern in those years—before the Eichmann trial—about the individual and his personal fate was quite limited.

In the 1960s, the activities in Israel to mark the Danish rescue reached their peak: a "Denmark Week" with multitude official events was celebrated twice, in 1963 to mark the 20th anniversary of the rescue and in 1968 to mark its 25th anniversary; in Beit HaKerem neighborhood of Jerusalem "Denmark Square" was inaugurated, in the center of which was placed a monument by the artist Rolf Roda Reilinger in the shape of a boat carrying Jews huddled between shards; in the Katamon neighborhood of Jerusalem a high school called "Denmark" was inaugurated; in primary schools throughout the country, classes were given about Denmark and its culture, and educators were asked to tell the pupils about the courage of the Danish nation and its initiative to save their Jews; children from a Danish fishing village that saved Jews in 1943 were invited to visit Ashkelon in the summer of 1964; three trees were planted in Yad Vashem in 1963, in honor of King Christian X, the Danish Resistance and the Danish people; the Danish ship *Astrid* that was used during the rescue operation to transfer the Jews to Sweden was docked in Haifa; and in the northern Kibbutz Neot Mordechai, the cornerstone for the foundation of a Danish folk high school (according to N. F. S. Grundtvig's vision) was laid, a project that ultimately did not come to fruition. It was during this decade, therefore, that the story of the rescue became a myth in Israeli Holocaust memory.

Between the Particular and the Universal

Over the years, the human-universal meaning inherent in the rescue has gained considerable representation. For example, Yad Vashem presented the Danish rescue not only as a choice of the non-Jewish individual to help Jews despite the risk of life that was involved during the Second World War, but also as a question of human moral values in general, whose focus is the thinking and autonomous person who does not drift with the current. The rescue, in general and in Denmark in particular, thus became one of the main educational topics that emerged as a lesson from the Holocaust. Indeed, to this day various museums that commemorate the Holocaust frequently mention not only the willingness of the Danes to help the persecuted Jews of their country, but also their commitment—even in dark and dangerous times—to preserve minority rights and to ensure civil equality.

This tendency is also noticeable in the Israeli education system. From an analysis of about two dozen history textbooks published since the 1950s, intended for high school pupils, two main characteristics emerge. The first characteristic is the use of the rescue as an example of proper human behavior, with a focus on the importance of democracy that enables it. Accordingly, the choice of the Danish people to act against the discrimination of the country's Jews, which is a corollary of their resolute position to protect the rights of minorities living among them, is what led to the overwhelming success of the rescue. The second characteristic is related to the way the rescue operation is described in the textbooks. For the most part, the descriptions include many inaccuracies, relevant facts are omitted, and the picture presented is partial and devoid of historical context. Interestingly, these characteristics are two sides of the same coin: in order to make the story of the rescue a unique example that should be emulated by the youth, it is necessary to simplify the historical event, avoid the complex context, and omit details that could dim the glow of the rescue. The representation of the rescue of Danish Jews in the education system also contributes, therefore, to its preservation as a myth in the Israeli Holocaust memory.

Layers of Commemoration

More than fifty years have passed between the inauguration of "Denmark Square" in Jerusalem in January 1962, and the inauguration of another "Denmark Square" in Hof HaCarmel in Haifa in June 2013. In both squares monuments of a boat are exhibited. The boat of the Danish fisherman Gilbert Lassen is the main exhibit in the "Resistance and Rescue" complex at the Yad Vashem Museum, and different boats appear in five out of the seven photographs shown there about the rescue in Denmark. Why did the fishing boat become the definitive symbol of the saving of Danish Jews? First, the boat symbolizes the general mobilization of the Danish people for their Jewish co-citizens: the willingness of the ordinary Dane to extend his hand to the persecuted Jews shows that not only King Christian X—a noble and uplifted figure, or members of the Resistance—brave and fearless fighters, but even the common man, embodied in the image of the fisherman, helped the Jews in the face of the Nazi threat. Second, the fishing boat is intrinsically intertwined with the "flowing water" motif, an ancient motif for describing feelings of freedom, liberty, and salvation. It seems, therefore, that the repeated use of the fishing boat symbol and the naming of the two squares that were erected in memory of the rescue after the entire Danish country, indicate that the many years that have passed have not changed anything in the meaning of the rescue event in the Israeli Holocaust memory. Maybe even the opposite: in the public landscape the mythical representation of the rescue is more solid and stable than ever.

Nevertheless, in other spheres at least two imperative changes can be found over the years. The first shift is related to the involvement of the Swedes. As early as October 8, 1943, during the peak of the sea crossing from Denmark to Sweden, the Israeli poet Nathan Alterman published in *Davar* newspaper a poem called "The Swedish Language." In the poem, Alterman brought up the miraculous Swedish opening of its borders to all Jewish refugees from Denmark, without conditions and without a quota, unlike the situation in the rest of the world. Interestingly, the Danes' contribution to the saving of the Jews was not mentioned in the poem even once. World public opinion as well appreciated at real time the Swedes for their extraordinary conduct (more than that of the Danes), and it was often used as an example of moral political behavior. In the 1960s, however, Sweden's place in the rescue representations in Israel and internationally gradually diminished: its contribution began to be noted, if at all, as marginal and mainly bureaucratic. Interestingly, in recent years Swedish diplomatic institutions have again started to highlight, on several occasions, Sweden's contribution to the rescue of Danish Jews.

The second shift is related to the developments in the status of survivors in Israeli society that have occurred over the years. Until the 1990s, the heroic ethos was applied to the Danish people, as a model for collective heroism. Since then, the image of the survivor, the story of the common Jew in occupied Denmark, began to stand out. This process, from collectivism to individualism, led to the focusing on the surviving Jew rather than the Danish nation, and to reducing the tendency to generalize and unify the experiences of all Danish Jews. In addition, the structure of the memorial events and their content has changed: compared to the first decades after the rescue, when the main purpose of the events' organizers was to thank the rescuers and their families, whether by inviting them to Israel or by holding events with their participation, in recent years the survivors and their families have become the main participants in the commemorative events, and in many cases they themselves are also the organizers.

Rescue and Politics

On August 10, 2001, journalist Tom Segev published an article in *Haaretz* newspaper called "When Gillon will invite guests." Although the stated subject of the article was the storm which broke out that summer surrounding the appointment of Carmi Gillon, former head of the Israeli General Security Service, as Israel's ambassador to Denmark, and the refusal of many Danish politicians to meet with him and even approve his appointment, most of the article dealt with the conduct of the Danes during the Second World War. In a nutshell, the article mentioned a number of studies conducted in the decade preceding its writing—mainly by Danish researchers—regarding the treatment of the country's Jews before, during and after the war: the Danish government's rejection of the request of tens of thousands of Jewish refugees for a transit visa or a residence permit between 1933 and 1939—and their positive response to only about 1500 of them; the high payment that some of the fishermen charged the Jews for transporting them by boat to Sweden; the economic losses that Danish Jews suffered upon their return to the country at the end of the war; the close economic cooperation between Nazi Germany and Denmark until the end of 1944; the volunteering of about 6000

Danish soldiers for the German Waffen SS and their participation in the fighting on the Eastern Front against the Soviet Union, including the murder of local Jews; and finally, the establishment of Danish factories throughout Eastern Europe and their operation through Jewish forced laborers. Although these studies have absolutely nothing to do regarding the appointment of Carmi Gillon as Israel's ambassador to Denmark, this article reveals one of the main features of the coverage of the Danish rescue in the Israeli press over the years: its use for the purposes of up-to-date interpretation of the political relationship between Denmark and Israel.

Since the establishment of the State of Israel in 1948, the vast majority of journalistic articles that have dealt with Danish-Israeli ties used the rescue operation as a lever to improve diplomatic relations. It was often claimed in the press during the 1950s and 1960s that it is only natural that a country that behaved in such an extraordinary manner toward their Jewish minority during the war would later also support the establishment of a national home for this minority, namely the State of Israel. Furthermore, the representation of the rescue in the press also served to tighten the relations between the long-lasting governance of Israeli Social Democratic party Mapai and the Danish Social Democratic party, at least until the late 1970s.

The deterioration of Danish-Israeli relations from the 1970s onwards led however to a more critical journalistic discourse in Israel toward Denmark. Israeli newspapers began to publish current studies, mainly translated from Danish, that criticized the cooperation between Denmark and Nazi Germany during the war, as well as testimonies of survivors from Denmark who presented a wide and varied spectrum of experiences—not always positive—regarding their personal rescue. In recent decades, it is possible to notice the formation of a more nuanced as well as complex attitude in the Israeli press toward the Danish rescue operation, an event that for many years was only mentioned positively in this media.

To sum up, the Danish rescue's multitude of commemoration patterns in Israeli Holocaust memory is an indication of its important status as an interpretive means connecting the past and the present. Starting in the 1950s, the State of Israel was the main factor that commemorated the rescue, and thus determined the nature and content of the memorial ceremonies. In the 1960s, the peak period in the formation of the rescue myth, the patterns of commemoration expanded: squares and monuments were erected all over the country, celebratory rallies were held and institutions were inaugurated to commemorate the rescue. The Danish request at that time from Yad Vashem, not to recognize individual Danes as "Righteous among the Nations" but the whole nation, the Resistance and King Christian X, a request that stemmed from their desire to emphasize the unity of the Danish people in opposition to Nazism,[7] fitted wonderfully with Israel's tendency to present the Danish case as a "ray of light in the darkness of the Holocaust," an extraordinary example that proves the rule.

In the last three decades, from the 1990s onwards, the buds of a new pattern can be detected, which affects, albeit partially, the prevailing commemoration. Researchers, journalists, and survivors try to challenge—through recent studies and personal stories—the accepted mythical representation of the rescue, and thus to bring it back to its natural dimension. However, these changes, which to a certain extent undermine the basic assumptions underlying the rescue story in the Israeli Holocaust memory, have not yet permeated the school textbooks, the public monumental landscape or the official-state representations of the rescue event. The grey, complex, and multifaceted truth about the rescue of Danish Jews in the Holocaust has not yet been fully revealed.

Notes

1. Orna Keren-Carmel, "Another Piece in the Puzzle: Denmark, Nazi Germany, and the Rescue of Danish Jewry", *Holocaust Studies* 24, no. 2 (2018), pp. 172–182.
2. "Welcome Prince of Denmark", *Haaretz*, 30 October, 2013.
3. Benjamin Slor to Mordechai Shenhabi, 28 June, 1947. Yad Vashem Archives, AM.1, file no. 94.
4. Dov Gerstensang. Yad Vashem Archives, O.3, file no. 12364.
5. Yehuda Kuper, *That's How it Was* (2003), p. 24. (Private publishing).
6. Leni Yahil, Introduction to *The Rescue of Danish Jewry—Test of a Democracy* (Jerusalem 1966), p. 15. Published in English in 1969.
7. Bjarke Følner, 'Memorials and Memorial Culture', in *Nothing to Speak of—Wartime Experiences of the Danish Jews 1943–1945*, eds. S. Lene Bak, B. Følner, P. Andersen Høg & J. Laursen (The Danish Jewish Museum 2011), p. 228.

CHAPTER 3

Ben Gurion, the Nordic Countries and the Neutral Bloc

Abstract This chapter sheds light on one of the less-known plans devised by Israeli Prime Minister David Ben Gurion, together with other senior officials at the Foreign Ministry, to get closer to (and maybe even join) the neutral bloc founded by the Nordic states at the start of the Cold War, as a means to alleviate Israel's international isolation. Throughout the chapter it becomes clear that the constructive relationship between the countries was founded on strong ties formed between members of the professional ranks, especially between the labor unions and cooperatives, and less on the ties formed between the politicians. Additionally, it focuses on these countries' shared yet unique foreign policy patterns and demonstrates the influence of common social-political values on the development of inter-state relations.

Keywords State isolation · Cold War · UN · Nordic cooperation · Aid to developing countries · Nordic neutral bloc

---

This chapter is based on my article published in Hebrew in *Cathedra*, 182 (October 2022), pp. 139–158. I would like to thank the editors of the journal for the permission to publish it here in English.

© The Author(s), under exclusive license to Springer Nature Switzerland AG 2024
O. Keren-Carmel, *Nordic Traces in Israel*,
https://doi.org/10.1007/978-3-031-75287-2_3

In 1952, one of the advisors of the Israeli Ministry of Foreign Affairs, Leo (Yehuda Pinchas) Cohen, wrote a letter to Abba Eban, Israel's envoy to the UN at the time, in which he presented a possible solution to Israel's international isolation:

> I am pondering the possibility of escaping our isolation at the UN and stabilizing our position by creating a 'progressive bloc' of some sort, within the UN. Experience taught us that on many issues we identify, in thought as well as in action, with a particular group of states in the UN – Canada, Australia, New Zealand, the Scandinavian states, the Netherlands and Uruguay. Moreover, from time to time, we received support from these countries on issues that are of importance to us. The question arises then: will we be able, in some way, to transform this measure of understanding and support into something more real and permanent, such as a stable arrangement for joint consultation and discussion on political issues that might be brought before the general assembly?[1]

Many political challenges troubled Prime Minister David Ben Gurion in the first decade following the establishment of the state of Israel. One of his main concerns was the international isolation of the young state. The Ministry of Foreign Affairs was relentlessly preoccupied with searching for solutions. This chapter sheds light on one of the less known plans devised by Ben Gurion and officials in the Ministry of Foreign Affairs, to deal with this challenging situation—the plan to make Israel a close ally of the Nordic countries.

The necessity to solidify Israel's international status became even more pressing as years went by, in order to get legitimation to its 1948 borders as well as to its basic right to self-defense. During the 1950s Israel was quite successful in reaching these goals in the African continent, while in Asia (except for Burma) it suffered numerous failures. In April 1955, for example, the Bandung conference in Indonesia was convened, bringing together the leaders of 29 states in Africa and Asia which had recently won their independence, and which together represented more than half of the world's population at the time. The conference marked the first step in the formation of the Non-Aligned States Organization, which was founded on an ideology of border-crossing solidarity, intended to counterbalance the political and economic inferiority of the Southern states relative to the Northern states. Its purpose was both to combat the implication of colonialism and to work toward calming the strained international atmosphere, in light of the emerging inter-bloc conflict. With the exception of Israel, almost all African and Asian states were invited to the conference. Israel being left out of the conference, combined with the escalating attacks in that period of Egyptian president Gamal Abdel Nasser on Israel's policy and the apparent failure of Ben Gurion's "periphery doctrine"—which called to develop close strategic alliances with non-Arab Muslim states in the Middle East—all intensified Israel's sense of isolation, and further stressed the need of finding other allies in the international arena.

The shadows of the Cold War, which broke out several years earlier, also encumbered Israel's choices.[2] In the complex international situation that emerged, each state had to take an unequivocal stand, and support either the Soviet Union or the United States. Like other heads of state at the time, Ben Gurion strained to avoid making a decision, desperately hoping to manage to keep Israel neutral within the escalating international conflict. This policy of non-alignment was a continuation of the organizing principle Ben Gurion followed in those years, aiming to preserve Israel's independence. Israel's unique situation mandated, in his opinion, that Israel be perceived as trustworthy when it comes to its concrete global intentions on the one hand, and that it avoids a clear public commitment with regard to the issues concerning the inter-bloc conflict on the other hand.[3] One of the solutions finally offered by Ben Gurion, and which conformed with Cohen's approach described earlier, was to establish a third, neutral bloc, which, in his own words, will be composed of "truly" peace seeking countries that will fight within the UN and outside of it for their common principles, such as maintaining cooperation between all nations regardless their regime, denouncing the use of violence, and abolishing all discrimination based on religion, race, and nationality. The four likely candidates to serve as the founders of such a bloc, Ben Gurion suggested, were Israel, Sweden, Burma, and Uruguay, among other reasons because they were not affiliated with either of the two super-powers.[4]

Why was Sweden among the four countries Ben Gurion suggested as potential founding members of his planned neutral bloc? One answer is that Sweden was already well-known, at that time, for successfully upholding an international neutral status.[5] But, a more significant reason was the exceptionally close relations that developed between Israel and Sweden since the end of the 1940s. Their close ties began with the endorsement of the UN partition plan of November 29, 1947, which was largely based on a report written by the Swedish Emil Sandström, Chairman of the United Nations Special Committee on Palestine (UNSCOP). Noteworthy, the assassination on September 17, 1948 of the first UN Mediator the Swede Count Folke Bernadotte by members of Israeli extremist "Lehi" organization did not have lasting consequences on Israeli-Swedish relations, though it did strain them for a while. Yet, above all, Israeli-Swedish cooperation during the 1950s was most prominent among the statist professional echelons. Theoretical and practical knowledge was exchanged between the countries relating to various social topics and welfare policies, resulting in mutual educational and professional expeditions of cooperatives and trade unions, in Israel as well as in the Nordic countries.

Nordic Cooperation

Having dissimilar security needs, after the Second World War each of the Nordic states made different strategic choices. Norway and Denmark, both occupied by Nazi Germany during the war, decided to become members of NATO, but refused to have neither nuclear weapons nor allied troops on their territories. Iceland, which from a strategic point of view was more Atlantic than North European, was the only NATO-aligned Nordic country with allied forces on a permanent peacetime basis on its territory. The Swedish security policy of non-alignment, aiming at neutrality in war, was supported by a comparatively strong defense. Finally, the security policy of Finland was conducted within the framework provided by the 1948 "Treaty of Friendship, Cooperation and Mutual Assistance" with the Soviet Union, which led to the forming of a special connection between the two states.

In spite of the major differences in their security policies, the Nordic states still desired to increase their mutual cooperation. A variety of initiatives for strengthening their ties were suggested by the governments of Sweden, Denmark, Norway, Iceland, and Finland, following the formation of the Nordic Council in 1952 (Finland joined in 1955). Some of these initiatives led to the creation of a common Nordic Labor market, a unified Nordic passport, and a unified social security system for all Nordic citizens. Additional initiatives for cooperation, mostly in cultural and political fields, got to be implemented following the formation in 1971 of the Nordic Council of Ministers, which was composed of committees of Nordic ministers on various policy areas. However, not all Nordic cooperation initiatives were successfully realized: the attempts to form a Nordic Security Pact in 1948–49 and an economic union (NORDEK) in 1968–1970 failed, among other reasons due to the pressure applied by the Soviet Union on Finland to withhold, and Denmark's joining of the European Union in 1973.

In conjunction with the Nordic unification efforts during the 1950s, a unique policy began to form among the Nordic states vis-a-vis the emerging inter-bloc conflict. Highlighted by their strategic geographical location, the purpose was to form an independent and neutral foreign policy, which is not influenced by the position of either superpower on the one side, and which strengthens the position of the Nordic states, as a unified bloc in the international arena, on the other side. Throughout the Cold War, and notwithstanding the difficult challenges it faced, this policy managed to keep the Nordic states out of the conflicts between the superpowers. At the same time, it allowed them to voice, based on existing circumstances, an independent foreign policy on various international issues.

Ben Gurion's abovementioned solution to ally itself with other neutral countries, with Sweden at the head, and thus to form an independent third bloc, was, however, fated to fail. Members of the Israeli government, as well as senior officials in the Ministry of Foreign Affairs and in Israel's delegations abroad, had an almost unanimous response to Ben Gurion's proposition: it is indeed a worthy idea, and forming relations with fellow "idealistic" countries could serve to pressure the Bandung states, but from a practical perspective, it is not implementable. It would be impossible to find counties willing to form a bloc with Israel. This is in particularly true, it was claimed, with regard to the Nordic countries: these were already members of the Nordic council and will not easily risk their neutral international status. Ben Gurion's proposal, so it seemed, was doomed.[6] Nevertheless, it was unlike Ben Gurion to give up on his vision. Despite the unenthusiastic responses to his plan, during the following years he worked tirelessly, together with Foreign Minister Golda Meir, to transform the Nordic countries into Israel's close allies.

During the continued crisis caused by Egyptian President Gamal Abdel Nasser's decision to close the Suez Canal to Israeli vessels and merchandise, Ben Gurion recognized his first chance to assess just how far the Nordic countries might go to support Israel. To test their willingness toward Israel, an envoy, Yosef Almogi—Israeli politician from Ben Gurion's party Mapai—was sent to several European countries in order to explain Israel's position and ask them to support, in every possible manner, the reopening of the Suez Canal.[7]

During the last two weeks of January 1957, the envoy visited Norway, Finland, Sweden, Denmark, the Netherlands, Belgium, Germany, and England, in this order. In Norway, he met with Haakon Lie, the Party Secretary of the Norwegian Labor Party, and the two agreed to work together toward a unanimous resolution from the seafarers' unions of the Scandinavian states, denouncing the Egyptian decision. Should they fail at that, they decided, they will ask for assistance from the Norwegian Union of Seafarers. This Norwegian union had a membership of around 60,000 seamen—at that time Norway had the world's third largest commercial fleet—and thus, it had great influence not only on issues relating to Norway's Economy but also to similar unions throughout Europe. During their meeting, Lie expressed his surprise that Israel does not sufficiently take advantage of the inherent potential of the Nordic professional unions and does not maintain sufficiently close ties with them. In addition, Lie recommended that the envoy Almogi would not include in his meetings with the Scandinavian unions any members of the Israeli Legation in Norway, because the unions treat the legation in a more reserved and official manner, while with an independent representative of the Histadrut (Israel's General Federation of Labor) "they are more loose and cordial in their treatment and show greater willingness to act."[8] The results of the meetings in Norway were highly satisfactory: both the Norwegian Foreign Minister and the Head of the Norwegian Union of Seafarers decided to express identification with Israel's demands, and in parallel they appealed on the subject to the UN (in addition to a separate, personal demand to UN's Secretary General, the Swedish Dag Hammarskjöld). They decided to publish the resolution in the Norwegian press and radio.

Finland was the next country the Israeli envoy visited. Thanks to the close ties established during that time between the trade unions in Israel and in Finland, as well as between the social democratic parties in both countries, the meeting between the envoy and the Head of the Union of Finnish Seafarers was described as exceptionally successful: the latter was well aware of the purpose of the envoy's visit and printed, with his own hands, the text for the desired resolution, in English and in Finnish, to be publicly published.[9]

In the next country the envoy visited, Sweden, he encountered a less excited response. The Swedish social democratic party responded to his request unenthusiastically, but thanks to the close ties between the Histadrut in Israel and the Swedish Workers' Union, the envoy managed to meet with the Head of the Swedish Union of Seafarers, a man "gifted with a warm heart and an un-Swedish sensitivity."[10] The Head of the union was well aware, in advance of their meeting, of the reason for the envoy's visit, and had prepared the text of the resolution, in Swedish, to be delivered to Dag Hammarskjöld, UN's Secretary-General. The envoy described as follows what transpired next:

> I innocently asked him to translate the resolution into English. He was insulted and told me: 'What do you think? Hammarskjöld is Swedish and he should read out the text in Swedish, so he doesn't think that upon rising to greatness, he may forget the language of his people, and the opinion of its workers.' I apologized, saying that I only asked for the English translation for myself, since, unfortunately, I don't speak Swedish. He calmed down and did as I asked.[11]

In Denmark, the last Nordic country the envoy visited, he met with the Head of the Union of Danish Seafarers, and as happened in Finland and Sweden before, the latter drafted, on the spot, a similar resolution in Danish to be delivered to the UN and published on local radio and newspapers.

Three main conclusions were derived from the envoy's tour of the Nordic countries. First, the heads of the trade unions in all Nordic countries expressed great interest in strengthening their ties with the Histadrut and with Israel's Labor Movement, both of which enjoyed at the time a positive international image and were treated with respect. The campaigning and lobbying of the Histadrut among the socialist movements in Europe, as well as among international institutions such as the UN, made it thus possible for Israel to receive, in time of need, wide support on various policy issues. Second, the importance attributed by the Nordic trade unions to strengthening the ties between themselves, as an aspect of Nordic cooperation, was stressed. The delegates continually consulted with their colleagues in neighboring Nordic countries, and coordinated the resolution in question among themselves. Lastly, the efforts to coordinate with the Nordic trade unions, as part of a larger goal to cooperate with the institutions setting the foreign policy in those countries, was a significant component of Israel's relationship with the Nordic states during those years.

About six months after the envoy's visit, the Director General of the Ministry of Foreign Affairs, Reuven Barkat, wished to begin promoting the plan to strengthen Israel's relationship with the Nordic countries. To this end, he asked Chaim Yahil, Israel's delegate to Sweden, Norway, and Iceland at the time (during his tenure, the diplomatic relations with Sweden were upgraded, and he became Israel's first ambassador to that country), to prepare a detailed review of the current positions of these countries toward Israel, and to suggest ways to strengthen Israel's relations with them.

In August 1957, Chaim Yahil sent his review, simultaneously, to Reuven Barkat and to Foreign Minister Golda Meir. The review contained two parts: Israel's relations with the social democratic parties in the Nordic states on the one hand, and its relations with the Nordic Labor movements, cooperatives, and trade unions, on the other hand. In terms of political relations, Yahil reported, Norway was the closest to Israel, followed by Denmark and then Sweden. Among the social democratic parties, there was generally a sympathizing and amicable attitude toward Israel, however, the degree of empathy varied according to specific circumstances and political considerations, as could be expected. For example, Yahil reported a certain cooling in the relations with Sweden, resulting from their disappointment in that the identity of Count Folke Bernadotte's assassins has not been revealed, and political considerations relating to the Suez War (October 1956) and its implications in terms of the Arab world.[12] The situation in Norway was similar: Finn Moe, a central foreign affairs ideologue in the Norwegian Labor Party, was convinced of Israel having the moral higher ground, but following the Suez War, he started expressing doubts with regard to the morality of its policy. At the same time, Yahil continued, the situation among the cooperatives, the Labor movements, and the trade unions in the Nordic countries was much better. There, Israel had many loyal friends, who were willing to prove their sympathy toward Israel not just in words, but also in actions. The common social democratic values of these institutions, in the Nordic countries as well as in Israel, served as a wide, solid, and common denominator, contributing thus to feelings of closeness and comradery. Given existing relations, Yahil suggested inviting a delegation from each Nordic country to visit Israel, for publicity purposes and as a means for strengthening the relations, and later on, sending Israeli delegations on reciprocal visits, during which the delegations will formulate their common understandings.

Aid Policy to Developing Countries

The aid policy of developed countries to developing countries is a phenomenon that dates back to the Second World War. The process of decolonization together with the political atmosphere that was formed with the outbreak of the Cold War, in which the involved parties aspired to create areas of influence all over the world within the framework of the inter-bloc struggle, led to the formulation of an extensive aid policy. Accordingly, the United Nations declared the 1960s a "decade of international development." The Nordic countries and Israel saw in providing aid to developing countries particular importance. In April 1960, the Council of the Socialist International met in Haifa, participated by ninety delegates from thirty countries, with the aim of discussing the aid that the International Socialist Movement should extend to developing countries:

> Two things can Socialists do (and will do) – to encourage governments to offer material support, both directly and through the United Nations: organize training and instruction. The second thing is done directly through the socialist parties: organizing a large seminar in India for south and south-east Asia, inviting socialist activists from Asian and African countries to Europe on an educational journey. The European socialists put all their knowledge to use in organizing workers, in political education, in social building, and all the knowledge of their colleagues, technical social knowledge, to use for the big mission – the complete freedom of mankind, politically, economically and socially. In every place a person might live: freedom for all – with no discrimination based on race or religion.[13]

The aid policy to the developing countries started taking shape in Israel in the mid-1950s,[14] several years earlier than in the Nordic states,[15] but they all had similar goals: they hoped to increase equality, solidarity, and peace between the "South" and the "North"; help developing states achieve economic and political independence; encourage the emergence of new markets in developing states; and improve their opening positions in future trade negotiations with the developing countries.[16]

As mentioned, in the first years of the Cold War, Ben Gurion was impressed with the success of the Nordic states to take an independent and neutral stance on foreign policy as well as to avoid being dragged into various local conflicts. Following, among others, the abovementioned detailed report by Chaim Yahil, Ben Gurion suggested replacing his original vision of establishing a neutral bloc by a vision of Israel's joining of the Nordic neutral bloc. The way to realize this plan was indeed complex, but showed great potential: Israel will become closer to the Nordic states by joining forces with them in the efforts to assist the developing countries, and this will eventually lead to Israel getting closer to the Nordic Council.[17]

Cooperation with the Nordic states, so believed Ben Gurion, could significantly strengthen Israel's aid policy to African countries, for four main reasons. First, the state of Israel was unable to cope, in the beginning of the 1960s, with the volume of requests for aid directed to it from (mainly) African countries. There was great concern that the political stronghold that Israel managed to acquire in these regions might fail, and that Israel might even be pushed aside by the larger powers. Second, partnering with the Nordic states, which were regarded as small and peaceful states, and whose past has—like Israel—not been tarnished by colonialism, could strengthen Israel's position among the developing states and undermine Arab counter-propaganda against Israel. Third, such cooperation would strengthen Israel's position among the Nordic states themselves, and would create a solid basis for reinforcing the relationship with them. As a result, the risk of Israel being isolated in the international arena will diminish. Finally, the cooperation of the Nordic states with Israel in offering aid was meant not only to allow for larger-scale solutions to the many humanitarian problems plaguing the developing counties, but also, at the same time, to provide them with an example of a willing cooperation between different sovereign states—one of the fundamental goals of international socialism.[18]

The first time Israel provided aid to a foreign country was in 1956, following the request of U Nu, the first Prime Minister of Burma, that Israel send agricultural specialists to build settlements for Burmese soldiers who were released from duty and looked for a place to settle. Shortly thereafter, the government of Ghana also requested assistance in structural planning, and Israel dispatched a team of engineers to train local professionals. In the following years, Israeli aid programs included training students from developing countries both in Israel and in their home countries, establishing learning centers, training medical teams, building clinics, and teaching community development, home economics, and public leadership. Israel viewed itself as especially suitable for the role of aid provider, as it was— like most of the developing countries—still a "country-in-the-making," and it possessed recent experience in solving similar difficulties. Moreover, the fact that Israel was a country with scarce natural resources and with a desert climate led it to search for original and cheap solutions to the challenges in the fields of agriculture and industry: it learned to exploit the most advanced technological developments in order to improve the efficiency of agriculture, development, and manufacturing. In the fields of chicken coops and irrigation systems, for example, Israel was considered a world leading expert. Israeli aid was in particular suitable for countries with a socialist regime—it focused on strengthening social institutions such as workers' unions, professional organizations and youth movements, and promoted industries that emphasized public responsibility. The Histadrut, in particular, was one of the most active institutions in Israel in providing aid.

The institution put in charge of formulating, leading, and implementing Israel's foreign aid policy was called "MASHAV"—the Center for International Cooperation (later on, its name was changed to "the Israeli Agency for Aid and International Cooperation"), and was formed within the Ministry of Foreign Affairs in 1958. In the budget year of 1959–1960, for example, MASHAV was already granted 34% of the overall yearly budget of the Ministry of Foreign Affairs.[19] The rate of increase in aid efforts was astounding: at the beginning of the 1960s, Israel has already extended aid to sixty-six countries around the world, especially those in South America, East Asia and Africa, and sent to these countries about 1800 Israeli experts for various periods of time.

In the Nordic states it was Viggo Kampmann, Denmark's Prime Minister in the years 1960–1962, who became the first statesman to try and expand the social democratic vision to the developing world. His being a visionary leader, who envisioned a borderless world based on international fraternity on the one hand, and a practical statesman, who was responsible for Denmark's economic policy as the country's former Finance Minister on the other hand, manifested the spirit of Nordic socialism in those years. The main problem facing the future of socialism, so he argued, was located outside the borders of Denmark, in the developing cooperation with other countries. In this arena, the Northern states play an important common role: introducing socialist ideas into international policy.[20] Kampmann and his social democratic party succeeded not only in creating in Denmark a unified front of willingness to increase the aid to developing countries, but also in setting the ground for the discussion on specific Danish aid programs. In order to fulfill the new policy, the Danish government appointed a temporary committee of five members (aid specialists and prominent figures in Danish industry and trade), who were given several responsibilities in the framework of the Danish aid program. The committee coordinated between the different aid institutions, conducted informational campaigns regarding the importance of aid programs, organized expeditions of Danish specialists to developing countries, received students from these countries who were granted scholarships for educational programs in Denmark, explored the opportunities for inter-Nordic cooperation and examined new suggestions for expanding the aid programs. Following Denmark, Sweden also decided to engage on the issue of aid to the developing countries. Two separate authorities were established there to handle aid matters: the foreign minister and his top advisors, who set the policy on the one hand, and an executive council called SIDA (Swedish International Development Authority) on the other hand. The two authorities acted in harmony most of the time, with minimal interference on behalf of the foreign minister and his advisors in matters of practical execution. The disagreements between them related mostly to issues such as the rate of action and the size of the budget, but not to the importance of the aid policy to Sweden. The scope of the aid of the Nordic countries, led by Sweden, Denmark, and Norway, to developing countries has increased significantly over the years: in the early 1960s they contributed to aid programs about 0.1% of their annual GDP, but after a decade they already stood at the top of the international donor table, providing one percent of their annual GDP, and sometimes even more, to aid programs.

Israel-the Nordic Countries-Africa

As instructed in 1959 by MASHAV, Israel's ambassadors to the Scandinavian states (mostly Chaim Yahil, followed by Arie Aroch, in Sweden, Reuven Barkat in Norway and Zvi Avnon in Denmark), began to discuss with the heads of local Labor movements the possibility of cooperation on aid programs to the developing countries in Africa. The plan of action suggested focusing on three related areas, aiming to benefit from the combined experience of different political systems. The first area included joint training of students from developing countries, with an emphasis on agriculture, whereas the theoretical background will be studied in a Scandinavian country and the field work will be done in Israel. The second area was the establishment of a joint corporation in one of the developing countries (in the field of construction, light industry, or textile), which will be run by the trade unions of the relevant countries. The third and last area dealt with the establishment of joint centers for professional training in the developing countries (centers for carpentry, welding, electricity, agro-mechanics, and so forth), in an attempt to train local technical teams quickly and efficiently.[21] Additional proposals for cooperation focused on the organization of further training for Israelis in the Nordic countries—and vice versa, and on the exchange of lecturers between the countries in areas such as rural planning, agricultural cooperation, industrial cooperation, and forestry.[22] Among other things, proposals were made to try to tighten cooperation with Nordic non-governmental organizations, such as the Danish social democratic women's organizations and the trade unions.[23]

Indeed, due to relentless efforts by the Israeli Ministry of Foreign Affairs, MASHAV and Israel's embassies in the Nordic countries, some cooperation between Israel and the Nordic states began to be realized. Starting in the early 1960s, Nordic experts arrived in Israel both in order to meet with their Israeli counterparts and in order to visit the various institutions participating in aid to developing countries, among others the Afro-Asian Institute in Tel Aviv, the Weizmann Institute of Science in Rehovot, the Mount Carmel Training Center in Haifa, the Hadassah Hospital in Jerusalem, the Center for International Agricultural Development Cooperation in Kibbutz Shfayim and the Volcani Center for Agricultural Research in Beit-Dagan. Upon arriving in Israel, they were given agricultural and educational tours by MASHAV and in the rest of the time, they visited and traveled the country with their hosts from the Histadrut and from Israel's Labor party Mapa"i. In the case of Sweden, even tighter cooperation was formed, mainly due to the initiatives of local women's organizations. SIDA, for example, granted a yearly budget to UNESCO (the UN's Education, Science and Culture organization), whereas one of the defined goals of that budget was to finance scholarships for women from Africa to train at the Mt. Carmel center in Haifa. Furthermore, throughout the years a variety of courses were given in Israel for training Swedish specialists, such as a course for agricultural planning given at the Weizmann Institute in April 1969, which was funded together by Sweden and the UN, and an irrigation course intended for water engineers, agronomists and hydrologists, given by the Volcani institute in the summer of 1969.

While the collaborations between the countries in the field of aid were already taking place, senior Israeli politicians tried to anchor the cooperation and its hopeful fruits also in the political field. The visit of Israeli

Minister of Trade and Industry, Pinchas Sapir, to the Nordic states in September 1960 provided the first opportunity for an in-depth discussion on the topic of cooperation in development aid, in an attempt to turn it from a mere idea to a political program. To that end, Sapir met in Sweden with the Deputy Chairman of the Trade Unions and with the Head of the Department of Heavy Industry of the Cooperative Movement, and the three acknowledged their positive attitude toward this subject. However, this subject was discussed in practical terms only during the next official visit in the Nordic countries of a senior Israeli political figure, namely Foreign Minister Golda Meir. After her successful visit to Africa three years earlier, Meir hoped that her visit to the Nordic countries in May 1961 will bring about an increase in the aid to Africa, by gaining the acceptance of the senior leadership of the Nordic countries, both at the party and the governmental level, to cooperate with Israel in extending aid to developing countries.[24] During her visit, Meir met with the foreign ministers and prime ministers of Denmark, Sweden, and Norway, and discussed with them the advancement of possible cooperation with Israel. For example, Meir suggested to the Norwegian Foreign Minister, Halvard Lange, to establish a mechanism for the exchange of views regarding aid operations in Africa, and the latter responded: "[t]here should not be a problem finding ways to exchange views, although it is not clear whether we will be able to found joint factories."[25] In Stockholm, the topic of extending joint aid was discussed with Prime Minister Tage Erlander in private, behind closed doors, and the summary of the discussion was not publicly published.[26] The reason for this was that during Meir's visit, the Nordic governments were still debating the best way for them to participate in aid and development programs to developing countries, and therefore refrained at the time from publicly announcing cooperation with Israel in the field.

Only a few months after Golda Meir's return, a string of visits by the Scandinavian prime ministers to Israel took place: Norway's Prime Minister Einar Gerhardsen arrived in Israel in November 1961, Denmark's Prime Minister Viggo Kampmann arrived in January 1962 and Sweden's Prime Minister Tage Erlander arrived in March 1962. These were the first three official state visits to Israel since its establishment. During the visits, specific plans were discussed to combine the resources of Israel and the Nordic states (separately with each state), in extending aid to developing countries. Finally, it was Ben Gurion's reciprocal visit to Sweden, Denmark, Norway, Finland, and Iceland in August 1962—his longest visit abroad as prime minister—during which the decision on joint Israeli-Nordic cooperation in extending aid to developing countries in Africa was supposed to be made.[27] Despite the many preparations which preceded Ben Gurion's visit to the Nordic countries and the many hopes set on it, ultimately, its results were far from satisfactory. All Nordic states refused to politically cooperate with Israel in extending aid to developing Africa, claiming that this is the role of the UN and its institutions, and not of individual states. The bold plan devised by Ben Gurion a few years earlier to strengthen relations with the Nordic neutral bloc through cooperation in the field of development aid, thus came to an end.

In contrast to the reasoning given at the time for the position of the Nordic countries, an analysis of Israeli Foreign Ministry documents from those years reveals two other reasons for the Nordic reluctance to cooperate with Israel in the field of development aid. It should be noted however that the analysis below is based on two long-term processes that in real time both the Israeli Ministry of Foreign Affairs and the political decision-makers in Israel were not sufficiently aware of their profound effects on the foreign relations of the Nordic countries.

The first reason has to do with the pressure the Arab countries began to apply in those years on Western countries politically or commercially cooperating with Israel. In his speech in the Swedish Parliament on November 7, 1973, Prime Minister Olof Palme officially announced for the first time that his country fears that oil production and its export will become a political weapon in the Middle East, as has already begun to happen in some cases, and that Sweden will also be affected by this in the future. Nevertheless, more than a decade before this speech the Swedish Foreign Ministry was already well aware of this possibly growing economic threat. Often, for example, concrete joint aid programs with Israel were canceled in Sweden "on orders from above," claiming that such cooperation might endanger Sweden's neutrality toward the Arab states.[28] Threats of boycott led Norway to also prefer economic cooperation with the United Arab Republic (the political union between Egypt and Syria from 1958 to 1961), at the expense of cooperating with the state of Israel.[29] Even Denmark, which responded most willingly to the idea of cooperating with Israel, succumbed to the growing Arab pressure and chilled its initial enthusiasm: following the visit of the Danish Prime Minister Kampmann to Israel, and his declaring, upon return to his country, of the possibility of cooperating with Israel on aid matters, the Danish government—as well as the Danish embassies in Arab countries—was flooded with grievances expressing the Arab countries' disdain of this proclamation.[30] In the words of Gunnar Seidenfaden, Head of the political department in the Danish Ministry of Foreign Affairs:

> Reality is, that we, as a small state whose way of life and tradition are determined to such a great extent by its foreign trade and seamanship, shall be very careful not to cause any disturbances to them. One Danish eye is always gazing at the butter we sell and on our ships that transport it, and that leads us to behave sometimes in an immoral manner. If someone amongst us would suggest cooperating with Israel, the East Asiatic Company will immediately awake, and so will all the rest, including the minister of trade, the minister of shipping and the minister of economics – and these are the determinative voices.[31]

Thus, despite the positive relations with Israel at the time, the Nordic states did not reciprocate Israel's eagerness to cooperate with them, as this would intensify their political and economic identification with Israel, a fact that had raised concerns internally, in terms of the Arab world's response. Furthermore, they were also concerned that their actions in developing countries will be affected down the road by possible complications that will surface between Israel and the Arab states, based on their already existing problems.

The second, and more decisive reason to the unwillingness of the Nordic states to cooperate with Israel on development aid, had to do with the inter-Nordic relationship. When the idea of extending aid to the developing countries began to form, in the late 1950s, each of the Nordic states looked for the best way for it to participate in the aid operations. Initially, they tended to limit their participation to annual contribution to the UN's aid programs and to ad hoc fundraising campaigns. This policy stemmed from the common perception at the time, according to which the activities of state-blocs in fields similar to those in which international institutions (such as the UN) are active, might create a precedent justifying similar activity on the part of the Soviet bloc. However, as time passed, public opinion in the Northern countries began to pressure their governments to play a more significant role in aid programs, and not only through UN institutions.[32] Indeed, within a short period of time the question of Sweden's future position among the developing countries stimulated lively debates in the government, in the social democratic party, in the trade unions, and within industrial circles. At the same time, Swedish government, together with the other Nordic governments, started to examine the feasibility of joint Nordic aid programs. These attempts were doomed for failure, initially, because Denmark and Norway suspected that Sweden was looking to profit at their expense, and to exploit their cooperation only until it completes its plans for expanding its national industry.[33] In April of 1962, however, a joint committee, comprising of delegates from Sweden, Denmark, Norway, Finland, and Iceland, recommended a unified Nordic aid effort rather than a separate effort by each country. The Nordic countries, which at first leaned clearly toward an independent national action, though within a general Nordic framework, finally changed their opinion. This was a result of their desire to give the committee's convention, which called for the strengthening of Nordic cooperation, a practical expression.[34]

In the short period of time between the visits of the three Scandinavian prime ministers to Israel (November 1961-March 1962) and Ben Gurion's reciprocal visit to the five Nordic countries (August 1962), things changed from end to end. First, Danish Prime Minister Kampmann, who expressed the most sincere enthusiasm for future cooperation with Israel, was forced to resign and was replaced by a prime minister who preferred a more limited approach in the field of international development aid; second, the relations between the Nordic countries and their desire to get closer to each other in the field of foreign policy led to a considerable tightening of relations between them, at the expense of cooperation with other countries. These changes caused in a short period of time for a sharp turn in Nordic foreign policy, resulting in a lack of interest in cooperation with countries outside their Nordic bloc in providing aid to developing countries.

To conclude, being a young, social democratic, and globally isolated state during the 1950s, led Israeli Prime Minister David Ben Gurion, together with other high-level officials in the Ministry of Foreign Affairs, to come up with a unique plan to improve Israel's position in the international arena: becoming closer to the Nordic states and the neutral bloc they formed in those years. The independent and neutral position that these states managed to cement in terms of their foreign policy, in addition to the social democratic values in terms of their internal policies, had a magnetic attraction on Ben Gurion, who hoped that through extensive cooperation between Israel and the Nordic states in extending aid to developing countries in Africa, conditions will ripen for them to come politically closer. However, to Israel's great disappointment, the Nordic connection turned out to be a Gordian knot. At the end of the day, the Nordic countries preferred to cooperate on aid programs with each other, and not with states outside their neutral bloc. Although Israel and the Nordic states had eventually some fruitful collaboration on aid issues, these were mainly the outcome of initiatives on the professional level, and not on the political level. The vast majority of these collaborations were the result of joint efforts of the Israeli and Nordic Labor movements, which strengthens the assumption, that the close relations during the 1950s and 1960s between Israel and the Nordic states were based more on the common values of the Labor movements than on political affinity.

On a more general note, this chapter sheds light on how the foreign policy patterns of social democratic countries were shaped and how they affected inter-state and multi-state relations. The tightening of foreign relations between countries with long-term social democratic rule after the Second World War—such as Bruno Kreisky in Austria, Willy Brandt in West Germany, and Olof Palme in Sweden—was based on connections created between the Labor movements of these countries, within the framework of training courses, tours and conventions of the Socialist International. These connections were an important basis for the rapprochement of these countries with each other and the creation of special relations between them, which sometimes resulted in significant successes in the international field.

Notes

1. L. Cohen to A. Eban, 8 April 1952, Yehoshua Freundlich (eds.), *Documents on the Foreign Policy of Israel*, 7 (Jerusalem 1992), p. 166.
2. For more see U. Bialer, 'State Building and Diplomacy: On the Historiography of Israel's Foreign Policy', *Cathedra*, 150 (December 2013), pp. 181–210. Interestingly, in this article, which comprehensively and meticulously reviews the foreign relations of the State of Israel in its early years, there is not a single mention of its close ties with the Nordic Countries.
3. U. Bialer, "Ben Gurion and Israel's Foreign Policy Orientation, 1948–1956", *Cathedra*, 43, (March 1987), p. 154.

4. D. Ben Gurion to the Foreign Minister, 28 June 1956, B. Gilad (ed.), *Documents on the Foreign Policy of Israel*, 11: January-October 1956 (Jerusalem 2008), pp. 518–519.
5. For more on Sweden's Cold War's Neutrality See for Example Aryo Makko, "Sweden, Europe, and the Cold War", *Journal of Cold War Studies*, 14, (Spring 2012), pp. 68–97.
6. See note 4.
7. An Examination of Norway's Considerations During the Suez Crisis is Found in H. Henriksen-Waage, "Norway and a Major International Crisis: Suez—the Very Difficult Case", *Diplomacy & Statecraft* 9, no. 3 (1998), pp. 211–241.
8. Yosef Almogi, 'Summarized Report from My Visit to Europe', p. 2, Israeli State Archives, חצ-3117/21.
9. Ibid., p. 4.
10. Ibid., p. 5.
11. Ibid.
12. C. Yahil to R. Barkat, Stockholm, 30 August 1957, p. 2. Israeli State Archives, חצ-3117/21.
13. This citation from the conference appeared in Meir Bareli, "The Task is still Major", *Davar*, May 6, 1960.
14. For more on Israel's aid policy to Africa, see: A. Oded, *Africa and Israel: a unique case in Israeli foreign relations*, London 2018, pp. 121–142; O. Ojo, Olusola, *Africa and Israel, Relations in Perspective*, Boulder, CO 1988; N. Chazan, 'Israel and Africa: Challenges for a New Era', *Israel and Africa: Assessing the Past, Envisioning the Future*, New York 2006, pp. 1–15; M. Curtis & S.A. Gitelson (eds.), *Israel and the Third World*, New Brunswick, NJ 1976; S. Decalo, *Israel and Africa: The Politics of Cooperation*, Philadelphia, PA 1970; Z. Levey, *Israel in Africa, 1956–1976*, Dordrecht 2012; J. Peters, *Israel and Africa: the Problematic Friendship*, London 1992.
15. For more on the Nordic Countries' aid policy to developing countries, especially from a historic and comparative perspective, see: T.B. Olesen, H. Pharo & K. Paaskesen (eds.), *Saints and Sinners. Official Development Aid and its Dynamics in a Historical and Comparative Perspective*, Oslo 2011; B. Oden, *The Africa Policies of the Nordic Countries and the Erosion of the Nordic Model: A Comparative* Study, (Discussion Paper, 55), Uppsala 2011; idem & L. Wohlgemuth, 'Swedish Development Cooperation Policy in an

International Perspective', *Perspectives*, 24 (2013): pp. 1–73; P. Hoebink & O. Stokke (eds.), *Perspectives on European Development Cooperation: Policy and Performance of Individual Donor Countries and the EU*, London and New York 2005; L. Engberg-Pedersen, 'The Future of Danish Aid: the Best of the Second-best?', N. Hvidt & H. Mouritzen (eds.), *Danish Foreign Policy Yearbook 2009*, Copenhagen 2009.

16. However, like the Israeli government, the Nordic governments were also suspected, from time to time, by citizens and politicians from all parts of the political spectrum, of 'neo-colonialist' intentions for their activities in the developing countries.

17. (Indirect) evidence for this plan can be found among others in the exchange of letters between the embassies in Scandinavia and the Ministry of Foreign Affairs in the early 1960s, and I will give a few examples. On December 5, Reuven Barkat, then already the Israeli ambassador to Norway, wrote to the director of the department for West Africa: 'I believe that we can, if we are interested in it, offer the Norwegians, and perhaps not only the Norwegians, to cooperate with Israel in the field of information and also in the field of economic action in West Africa. Such a proposal, if it is formulated in a matter-of-fact and purposeful manner, may perhaps be accepted by the Norwegian government. Of course, if my opinion is indeed accepted—this may help both to strengthen the ties between us and Norway and to the coordination and cooperation between us and Norway in the field of Africa' (State Archives, חצ-3335/51). On January 2, 1961, Barkat wrote to the director of the Department for Western Europe at the Ministry of Foreign Affairs: 'During my days in Norway, I devoted a lot of time, energy and effort to motivating the Norwegian decision-makers to action and greater interest in the countries of Asia and Africa and in plans for cooperation, action - which resulted in the fact that the governing party added a special section on aid to underdeveloped countries in which our influence is clear' (ibid.); On February 20, 1961, Aroch, Israel's ambassador to Sweden, wrote to the director of the department for West Africa at the Ministry of Foreign Affairs: 'The idea of cooperation as mentioned above [between the cooperative movements of Israel and Sweden in Africa] was first brought up almost two years ago. On various occasions it was used as a topic for conversations [...] with the leaders of the labor movement

here and I discussed it in fact from the day I arrived here. One of the suitable opportunities for a practical conversation was during Minister Sapir's visit here, when he met, especially for this purpose, with Blumgren, Chairman of the Trade Unions and Geyer's deputy [Arne Geyer was at the time the president of the trade unions in Sweden] and Gilberg, Head of the department of heavy industry of the Cooperative Movement. The two confirmed their positive attitude to the matter. About two and a half months ago, I spoke about it again with Arne Geyer. […] On this occasion I came to know again that Geyer treats the proposal in all seriousness. It was clear that various developments in public opinion, the movement and the Swedish public, in recent times, strengthened his sympathy for the idea even more. […] There is of course no need to expand on the benefits that could emerge for us as a collaborator' (ibid).

18. For more on this last argument see G. Myrdal, 'Beyond the Welfare State', S. Wurm and M. Avizohar, eds. *An Anthology of Contemporary Socialist Thought 1939–1965*, 1 (Tel Aviv 1965), pp. 465–469.
19. In comparison, in the year 2019 MASHAV'S's budget was only 0.19% from the overall Foreign Ministry's budget (Pages/Reports/3285–14.aspx?AspxAutoDetectCookieSupport = 1, and also: https://next.obudget.org/i/budget/0009510306/2019. Retrieved on 18.7.2021).
10. V. Kampmann, 'An Outline for an Ideological Platform', in *An Anthology of Contemporary Socialist Thought 1939–1965*, eds. S. Wurm & M. Avizohar, 1 (Tel Aviv 1965), p. 481.
21. Further suggestions on joint Israeli-Nordic aid programs to Africa can be found in the Israeli State Archives, חצ-3335/51.
22. C. Hareli to the Foreign Minister, 17 July 1965(?), Israeli State Archives, חצ-2880/6.
23. Ibid.
24. Israeli Embassy in Stockholm to the Israeli Ministry of Foreign Affairs, 9 May 1961, Israeli State Archives, חצ-4323/3.
25. R. Barkat to Bendor, 20 May 1961, Israeli State Archives, חצ-4323/3.
26. Israeli Embassy in Stockholm to the Israeli Ministry of Foreign Affairs, 9 May 1961, Israeli State Archives, חצ-4323/3.

27. Nevertheless, not everyone in Israel appreciated Ben Gurion's vision of forming closer ties with the Nordic states. In the Communist newspaper *Kol Haam*, for example, Ben Gurion's ambitions were reported as daydreaming: "it is an altogether not modest goal, but a goal that proves the megalomania of its initiator, which is neither compatible with the power nor the interests of Israel" (B. Balti, 'Ben Gurion in Scandinavia', *Kol Haam*, 31 August, 1962).
28. M. Bitan to MASHAV, 27 December 1963, Israeli State Archives, חצ-1911/4.
29. R. Barkat, to the Financial Department, 21 March 1961, Israeli State Archives, חצ-253/13.
30. H. Levin to the Director of MASHAV, 20 November 1962, Israeli States Archives, חצ-1905/2.
31. H. Levin to the Director of MAAR (Western Europe department), 4 April 1962, Israeli State Archives, חצ-1905/2.
32. A. Aroch to the Director of MAAR, 18 November 1960. Appendix. Translated by the Israeli Embassy in Stockholm, Israeli State Archives, חצ-3335/51.
33. Ibid.
34. H. Levin to E. Avriel, 17 April 1962, Israeli State Archives, חצ-1906/3.

CHAPTER 4

Nordic Wooden Huts and Israeli Public Housing

Abstract This chapter presents the considerable Nordic influence on Israeli housing solutions in the 1950s. Following the need for rapid housing solutions resulting from the steep demographical rise after the establishment of the Israeli state in 1948, thousands of imported Nordic wooden huts became part of the Israeli landscape. What prompted Israel to import those huts specifically? The chapter examines the considerable contribution of the Nordic huts, along with all their challenges, to the building of the newly established Israeli state from the first purchase in 1946 to the nostalgic commemoration of the huts nowadays.

Keywords Wooden huts · Public housing · Housing shortage · Jewish agency · Ma'abarot (transit camps)

Wooden huts, and especially Nordic wooden huts, have been part of the Jewish settlements' landscape in Palestine for over a century. The first wooden hut was probably the "Sverdlov hut" that was erected in Gedera in 1888, the days of the first Aliyah (Jewish immigration wave), for the benefit of the new Jewish settlers there. Over the years, the wooden huts became a visual symbol for the extensive transfers that Jews, among others, experienced during the first half of the twentieth century throughout Europe, Africa, and the Middle East. With the founding of

© The Author(s), under exclusive license to Springer Nature Switzerland AG 2024
O. Keren-Carmel, *Nordic Traces in Israel*,
https://doi.org/10.1007/978-3-031-75287-2_4

Israel in 1948, a unique state dimension was added to the wooden hut. The first Prime Minister David Ben Gurion and his wife Pola established their residence in 1953 in a wooden hut in Sde Boker in the Negev, while the country's second president, Yitzhak Ben Zvi, and his wife Rachel Yanait, built their residence in a wooden hut as well, in the same year, in the Rehavia neighborhood of Jerusalem. For both couples, living in wooden huts—a modest accommodation—embodied the socialist values upon which the young country was built. To this day, these two wooden huts, together with dozens of other wooden huts throughout Israel, are a nostalgic testimony to the early days of the country, and to the pioneering spirit of those who lived in them.

After the Second World War ended, the decision-makers of the Jewish population in Palestine came to understand that they were facing the absorption of a mass immigration ("the 100,000 immigration," as they narrowly expected at the time its future scope). Only then did the necessity of the wooden huts as a quick housing solution take on an urgent dimension. Between July 1948 and July 1951, the peak period of immigration to Israel, between 10,000 and 31,000 immigrants arrived each month, so that in three years the Jewish population in the country doubled from 650,000 to 1,322,000.[1] The immigrants were divided into two: the "sheerit hapleta" (Holocaust survivors), who came from the displaced persons camps in Western Europe and from the British detention camps in Cyprus, and the Jewish communities in Muslim countries in Asia and Africa, whose fear of persecution following the establishment of the State of Israel led to the need for their immediate evacuation. About 24,000 immigrants came from the detention camps in Cyprus, about 330,000 from the displaced persons camps and other European countries, and about 238,000 from (mainly) Iraq, Yemen, and Tunisia. In those years, the rate of immigrants per 1000 inhabitants to Israel was higher than the rate during the peak periods of immigration to countries such as Argentina, Canada, and the United States. In 1951, however, there was a significant turning point in the scope of immigration which led to a drop in the number of immigrants and in the years 1952–3 less than 1000 immigrants arrived in Israel every month. This trend stopped in 1955, when a certain increase began to be registered again, but it never returned to the immigration level of the years 1951–1948.

Housing Shortage

Even before the arrival of the masses of immigrants, it was clear that the main shortage would be in the area of housing. The Jewish Agency, in its role as responsible for the absorption of the new immigrants, started to search for temporary housing solutions and appointed the director of its technical department, the engineer Jaakov Reiser (1893–1974), to handle the issue. Reiser's initial idea was to import wooden huts ready for immediate occupancy, but an examination of the high costs of such huts led him to consider a different idea: assuming that raw wood can be obtained at a reasonable price, local industrial production of huts would be preferable. The construction cost will be lower than the import price of ready-made huts, and it will be possible, during their construction, to adapt them more precisely to the local needs and weather conditions. The problem, he claimed, lied in the difficulty of purchasing raw wood for construction—a resource that was in short supply after the Second World War—as well as the preference of commercial companies to sell ready-made huts rather than raw wood, since the net profit for the former was much higher. The solution he proposed, therefore, was a combined one: buying ready-made huts in the smallest amount necessary in order to obtain the maximum amount of raw wood for construction.[2] Although Reiser's proposal was accepted,[3] the need to find even faster housing solutions decided against it soon after.

The purchase of the wooden huts was done through parallel agreements. The Jewish Agency signed at the same time procurement contracts with foreign governments and foreign companies, and contracts with Israeli companies such as "Pertschonok Timber & Building Materials," "Timber Stores Ltd" and the "Scandinavian Timber & Trade Agency," which sold the imports that arrived in Israel to the local market, mainly to construction and housing companies such as Solel Bone and Amidar.[4] The purchase was made in creative ways, including quite complex ones. In one of the transactions, for example, the Jewish Agency received a loan from an American fruit export company for $2,300,000 for a period of 3–4 years. In return for the loan, the Agency bought prefabricated wooden huts and a certain percentage of raw wood from Sweden, for which the American company paid by exporting fruit on its behalf to Sweden.[5]

Nevertheless, the division of labor between the Jewish Agency and the Israeli government institutions that assisted in the purchase and construction of the wooden huts did not work smoothly, to say the least. In its purchase of wooden huts in the Nordic countries, for example, the Jewish Agency operated as a private entity, meaning it did not use an auction policy, rather buying all the wooden huts from a single Swedish company. Other companies that tried to conduct business relations with the Jewish Agency, and even offered wooden huts at much lower prices, were rejected outright. It was however the Israeli delegation in Sweden (at the time it was not yet recognized as an embassy), to which the criticism and complaints were directed, both by local industrialists who were denied the opportunity to offer their goods to the Jewish Agency, and by officials in the Swedish government who often wondered about the puzzling way of the Jewish Agency's doing business. The Israeli delegation not only suffered from a severe lack of information about the activities of the Jewish Agency, since the latter refused to inform it about its plans and purchases in Sweden, but also had difficulties in explaining the Jewish Agency's decisions satisfactorily. The commercial attaché of the delegation complained, for example, that the evasion of engineer Reiser from the Jewish Agency from meeting with other suppliers does not add to the good name of Israel: "In every contact, we are asked the same question: why is the purchase directed to only one pipe [...]? We were asked this question at the Swedish Ministry of Foreign Affairs, the Swedish Ministry of Trade, the various suppliers, Jews of all kinds, all ask whether everything is conducted here as it should."[6]

Beyond the lack of cooperation between the Israeli state bodies and the Jewish Agency, the conflict between them revolved around an even more fundamental issue. While the Jewish Agency tried to take care of quick housing solutions using the money from the lenders that it was collected ("Milve"), the Israeli delegation in Sweden, and especially its commercial department, was interested in increasing the scope of Israel's trade with Sweden through the commercial contracts signed between the two countries every year. Often, these desires collided in the field of purchasing the wooden huts:

> There is no doubt, and this is evident at every step, that the large purchases here by the Agency and the KKL (about 4.5 million dollars in one year) were an important factor in the Swedes' refusal to enter into a payment agreement. If there had been more of a match between the purchases of the aforementioned institutions and the economic operations of the Israeli delegation, there is no doubt that the Swedes would have accepted our proposal and perhaps also be inclined to additional loans [...]. Buying

houses for 4.5 million dollars is an important event in this industry in Sweden and the pressure that the manufacturers would have exerted on their government could have been an important tool for us. Unfortunately, this is not the case.[7]

In addition, the significant decrease in the volume of trade between Sweden and Israel—from 28 million Swedish kroner in 1953 to just under 12 million Swedish kroner in 1954—was primarily due to the termination of the transaction for the purchase of wooden huts, and testified to its importance to the trade relations between Israel and Sweden in those years.

The situation in Finland was similar. In 1949, the Jewish Agency, through engineer Reiser, decided to purchase large-scale wooden huts from Finland. In exchange for the Agency's promises, the Finnish government agreed to sign a trade agreement with the State of Israel in which it will be granted the status of a first-priority country. Immediately after the signing of the commercial agreement, and Israel's acceptance of the preferential status as a first-priority country, negotiations between the Jewish Agency and the Finns began. However, after some time the negotiations reached an impasse and the Jewish Agency decided to cancel the purchase of the wooden huts. A complex diplomatic crisis began to take shape.[8] The Israeli government managed to avoid it at the last minute: it purchased from Finland the 350 wooden huts in place of the Jewish Agency and paid for them from its own budget.[9]

The mutual complaints of the Jewish Agency and the state institutions often reached Finance Minister Levi Eshkol, for whom the decision between the parties was not an easy task.[10] The reason for this was that Eshkol held two positions simultaneously, which sometimes conflicted. In his first hat, Eshkol was Minister of Finance between the years 1952–1963, but in his other hat he was a member of the Jewish Agency's management, serving as its treasurer in the years 1949–1951 and as head of the settlement department in the years 1948–1963. During this term, he oversaw the establishment of 371 new settlements and the expansion of about 60 existing settlements throughout Israel. In the decisions that Eshkol had to make in disputes between state bodies and the Jewish Agency, he sided, in most cases, with the Jewish Agency. He believed that although the Jewish Agency often operated apart from the state institutions, and this conduct led to a real conflict of interest in the economic field, finding a solution to the housing crisis that existed in the young country was more urgent.[11] However, he had another important reason. The Jewish Agency's preference to work with only one supplier in Sweden, chosen without a tender, was received with understanding by Eshkol, who was himself, as Minister of Finance, using this same supplier to make extensive purchases of weapons for the IDF.[12] It is interesting though to note that in those years Eshkol also had a third hat: between 1949 and 1953 he headed the board of directors of the abovementioned Amidar, a private company which was involved in the construction of public housing. Therefore, he was probably participating in the transfer of the Jewish Agency's role in the area of housing solutions to Amidar, which occurred in 1952.[13] Since then Amidar was responsible for both the construction of the "Amidar neighborhoods" and of their maintenance along the years.[14]

THE NORDIC WOODEN HUT

It is unfeasible today to trace the exact number of wooden huts purchased from the Nordic countries in the early days of Israel. A general estimate, however, is about 20,000 wooden huts for residences and another 1500 wooden huts for public institutions.[15] The Nordic wooden huts, unlike those bought for example in Austria, Germany, Holland, United States, or Belgium, included unique features that made them stand out in the Israeli landscape. The Finnish wooden hut, for example, came in two models. Both were designed to house two families (in each hut), and the difference between them was expressed in the area of each of the housing units. The small model included two housing units measuring 28 square meters each, including a living room, a kitchen and a bathroom, while the large model included two housing units measuring 35 square meters each, including two rooms, a kitchen, and a bathroom. The height of the hut was 2.5 meters, and it weighed about 5 tons. All wooden huts included a floor, ceiling, roof, exterior and interior walls, doors, windows, frames, and screws. The price of a unit in the small model was $940, while a unit in the large model cost $1115 (before shipping).[16]

The purchase of thousands of wooden huts in the late 1940s and early 1950s became one of the most expensive and complicated transactions that the young state of Israel made with foreign countries. As a result, quite a few challenges and problems also emerged. The first problem was discovered already at the transportation stage. Most of the transportation from Northern Europe, until the purchase of the wooden huts, was done by two shipping companies, one from Sweden and one from Finland, both represented at the time by the Israel Scandinavian Maritime Agency. However, the transportation of the wooden huts was a complex operation. It was only possible during several months of the year—when the ports in Northern Europe were not full of ice, and a lot of storage space was required inside the ships as well as professional skills in loading and unloading the wooden panels—which were heavy and large. Accordingly, the cost of transportation was considerable. As the rate of purchase of the wooden huts increased, Israel began to look for cheaper transport solutions, mainly by loading them on "hitchhiker" ships that were on their way to the port of Haifa anyway. When the Israel Scandinavian Maritime Agency discovered this, a crisis broke out, which was resolved only after a considerable amount of time and many efforts on behalf of the Israeli Ministry of Labor.

The second problem was both expected and surprising. Wood, as it turns out, is a flammable material. More than once the wood shipments caught fire while on their way to Israel, but most of the fires occurred after the huts were set up on the ground. The Minister of Labor at the time, Golda Meir, often spoke about this in various forums:

> I fear to death when I see concentrations of wooden buildings, and the tenants using primos and other oil machines, when they are not used to these devices, I think it is a miracle that no major disasters have happened yet, it does not mean that I am sure that it could not happen in the future.[17]

As far as this research was able to verify, no major disasters occurred, but fires of wooden huts—and subsequently harmed tenants—were an integral part of this housing solution. Between the years 1947 and 1969, dozens of reports were published in Israeli newspapers, describing wooden huts that burned down completely, all over the country, as a corollary of short circuits, oil lamps and wicks falling, lightning strikes, spread of nearby wildfires, and sometimes even deliberate arson. Following the accumulated experience, the Division for Public Works began to demand that, at the same time as buying wooden huts, the state must also purchase fire extinguishers for them.[18]

The Nordic wooden huts were used as a temporary housing solution both for new immigrants who had just arrived in Israel and for the residents of transit camps ("Maabarot") who wanted to improve their living conditions. Depending on the location of the settlement, a payment of between 100 Israeli Pound (IP) and 300 IP was required for a wooden hut, an amount that was used as a down payment on the future rent. Alternatively, if there was an interest, the wooden hut could be purchased for 600 IP, and the remaining amount was paid later through a government mortgage.

The Nordic wooden huts were erected all over Israel: in immigrant settlements, kibbutzim, moshavim, and new neighborhoods in the cities. The majority of wooden huts were used for immigrant residences, while a minority was used for various public needs such as clinics, kindergartens, secretaries, telephone operators, post offices, and more. In 1949, for example, 560 housing units in Swedish wooden huts were built in Acre, 200 in Herzliya, 120 in Petach-Tikva, 100 in Nahariya,[19] between 100 and 200 in Kfar Ata, 100 in Binyamin, 200 in Givat Olga,[20] 25 in Moshav Kadima, and 5 in the workers camp "Beit Shlomo Organization" near Kfar Saba.[21]

However, not all the Nordic wooden huts that arrived in Israel were purchased by the Jewish Agency, some came as a contribution to the building of the country from foreign donors. Two significant donations even made it possible to build new rural settlements.[22] For example, the Swedish association "Swedish-Israel Aid" managed to raise over one million Swedish kroner from various parties in the Swedish government, the parliament, the Social Democratic Party, labor unions, the Jewish community, and especially the Lutheran Church and other religious organizations in Sweden, with which they bought 75 wooden huts, including the sending of a Swedish engineer who took care of their construction on the ground. Through this donation, in 1949, moshav Kfar Ahim was established, which is located near Kastina junction, and where Holocaust survivors from Eastern Europe, mainly Romania, Poland, and Hungary, could be settled. The Swedish wooden huts have been an essential part of Kfar Achim's landscape for many decades.[23]

The second moshav established thanks to the donation of wooden huts, this time from Norway, is called Yanuv and is located in the Sharon plain. The circumstances of this donation are of particularly tragic circumstances, and lie in the biggest air accident up to that time in Norway. On November 20, 1949, a passenger plane that took off from Tunis crashed near Oslo and its passengers, 27 Jewish children from Tunis and Morocco, three companions, and four crew members, perished. Amazingly, one 11-year-old boy—Yitzhak Allal—survived the crash unharmed. The purpose of the trip was to allow the children to stay in Norway for a few months before immigrating to Israel in order to prepare for their new lives and learn Hebrew, while their families were supposed to follow them later on directly to Israel. The Norwegian public, of all its layers, was extremely shaken by the accident. The Norwegian Labor Party, headed by General Secretary Håkon Lie, decided to donate 50 wooden huts to Israel in order to build a new settlement in memory of the children, companions, and staff members who perished. In this way, they believed, they would be commemorated in a way that would also benefit the building of the new state. Unfortunately, the ship that brought the wooden huts to Israel caught fire, and they all burned down. The Norwegian Labor Party did not give up and a short time later 50 new wooden huts were sent to Israel, which reached their destination safely.[24] In one of the first wooden huts that were built, the child survivor Yitzhak Allal moved in, together with his family. *Maariv* newspaper reported the event as follows: "The Norwegians decided on a nationwide initiative to establish a kibbutz in memory of the plane's victims. They said - and they did. For some reason, the kibbutz became a moshav, built entirely of shiny and polished Swedish huts [should be Norwegian huts - O.K.C]. The name of the moshav is Yanuv."[25]

Nordic Wooden Huts as Public Buildings

One of Israel's central, expensive, and most complex projects in its early years was the establishment of three hospitals. Chaim Sheba, the Director General of the Ministry of Health in 1950–1952, decided to use Finnish huts for this project, and declared it "the most important achievement of our efforts aimed at providing hospitalization in pre-planned hospitals at reasonable prices and in a relatively short period of time."[26]

In August 1951, the Ministry of Health received official approval for the purchase and construction on the ground of Finnish wooden huts for the purposes of establishing three medical centers: one in Nahariya, one in Poriya, and one in Tzrifin (later renamed Assaf Harofeh and today the Shamir Medical Center).[27] Funding for the project came from two sources: $200,000 from the Jewish Agency and $100,000 from the rehabilitation funds of the disabled from the War of Independence, founded by Vera Weizmann—a doctor and the wife of Chaim Weizmann, the first president of the State of Israel.[28] Chaim Sheba appointed the engineer Gad Asher as the chief architect of the project and the Israeli Jacob

A. Lewison Company to mediate in the purchase of the wooden huts between the Finnish company Puutalo Oy and the Israeli Ministry of Health.

The reasons for preferring wooden huts as buildings for the new hospitals were varied. First, the speed of construction. While planning and construction of permanent buildings takes several years, the planning, transportation, and construction of wooden huts took only a few months. Secondly, although wooden huts increased the running expenses due to the longer distances that the staff members had to cover (compared to high-rise buildings), on the other hand, it made it possible to give up elevator services altogether, thus cutting electricity expenses and also preventing a possible paralysis of the activity due to power outages. The third reason was the possibility of adding more wooden huts, in the future, according to the expansion of each medical center. For example, at the beginning the Rural Medical Center Poriya, as it was called at the time, was designed to include 19 wooden huts, where each hut functioned as a separate department. It had three surgical huts, three internal medicine huts, three children's huts, a maternity hut, a family health center hut, an operation hut, an X-ray hut, a day-hospitalization hut, a kitchen hut, a warehouse hut, a laboratory hut, a reception hut, and an administration hut. Already at the construction stage, the option to add further huts in the future was planned. In order to reduce construction costs, all the wooden huts were designed as uniform units. With the exception of the flooring, roofs, and air conditioning system—which were made in Israel—all other construction components, including electricity and sanitation, came from Finland. At the special instruction of engineer Gad Asher, also a high number of fire extinguishers arrived.

After careful planning, adjustments, procurement, and transport, the wooden huts for the three hospitals arrived at the port of Haifa in 1952, stored in tens of thousands of large and small packages. Along with them, arrived 22 further wooden huts designed to house the hospital workers and doctors.[29] However, at this stage the project encountered its most complicated obstacle. In November 1951, a few months before the arrival of the wooden huts, Chaim Sheba claimed that once they arrived it would be possible to transport them directly to their location and begin their construction on the ground: in Nahariya all that was left was to ask the accountant general to allow the state to purchase the area intended for the hospital from the custodian of German property in Israel; in Tzrifin only final approval from the army was required; and in Poriya the negotiations for the lease of the land from the state had just ended.[30] The reality on the ground, however, turned out to be much more complex. In a letter to Health Minister Yosef Burg, engineer Gad Asher described the situation after the arrival of the wooden huts to Israel: in Nahariya, so many administrative difficulties were piled up on the location of the construction of the hospital, that it was decided to examine an alternative location in the nearby city of Acre; in Tzrifin, they were still waiting for a final answer from the army; and in Poriya - the construction division was strongly opposed to the construction of a hospital in the area of its authority, and therefore avoided giving approval. The non-allocation of the land caused repeated postponements in the construction of the three hospitals, since without detailed land plans it was not possible to prepare the infrastructure for electricity and plumbing that were required for the construction of the wooden huts.[31] The many problems that arose reached the government, where, for example, Knesset member Idov Cohen from the Progressive Party complained that Minister of Labor Golda Meir did not detail, in her review on the housing crisis, the "failures and difficulties we encountered, the waste and unfortunate losses: for example, the fact that there was both a budget and huts, but we wasted time due to our inability to overcome problems of land planning."[32] Only half a year after the arrival of the wooden huts in Israel, the approvals required for the project were received and construction work began.

From Temporary Housing Solution to Nostalgic Asset

The Nordic wooden hut, popularly called in Israel as the "Swedish hut" or the "Finnish hut," is part of the national landscape—on the ground as well as in the collective memory, to this day. On the website *Nostalgia Online*, which was established by the Council for the Promotion of Israeli Heritage, the term "Swedish Hut" is defined as follows:

> The 'aristocrats' of the various huts that arrived in the kibbutzim in the 1950s were the Swedish huts that came from... Sweden. These were intended for living in luxurious conditions at the time: two large rooms in each housing unit, kitchenette, bathroom, wooden floor, large windows etc. As the years went by and the kibbutz members moved to built houses, the kibbutz huts were increasingly used as temporary residences

for workers, training groups, volunteers who came to aid the kibbutzim after the 1967 war (among them, of course, the Swedish female volunteers whose reputation for beauty and sex made a magnificent chapter in the history of the kibbutz...), the soldiers of the kibbutz, etc. Some of the huts in each kibbutz were also used as various internal institutions - which led to their customary local characterization (the secretariat's hut, the building's hut, the post office's hut, the studio hut, etc.), and some turned into various warehouses, which in many kibbutzim are used in this capacity to this day.[33]

Over the years, the fate of the wooden huts was divided into two. The wooden huts intended for public needs were sent to peripheral settlements, and then replaced by permanent buildings. Thus, for example, in 1954, the wooden huts of the three mentioned hospitals were de- and reconstructed in distant medical centers: the huts from Poriya were sent to the health center in Kiryat Shmona, to MALBEN (Institutions for the care of handicapped and disabled immigrants) in Nahariya and to the Hadassah hospital in Be'er Sheva; the wooden huts from Tzrifin were sent to Tel Hashomer Hospital.[34] Nevertheless, the ravages of the Mediterranean weather, the perishable materials of the huts and the precision required in their reassembly led to considerable challenges in their re-erection, and they were therefore not always successful. The fate of the wooden huts used for residence, however, was better. In 1970, 5093 families still lived in wooden huts,[35] and throughout the 1980s, quite a few ads could still be found in the Israeli press asking to sell, or buy, wooden huts for residential purposes. This is how, for example, the history of the wooden huts in Kibbutz Barkai was described:

> In the 1950s, huts from Sweden arrived in Israel and in the kibbutzim, hence the name "Swedish hut". The great advantages of the Swedish hut were the speed and ease of assembly, the disadvantages: incompatibility with the climatic conditions in the country and the speed and ease of assembly! Yes, the advantages became disadvantages because it took away work from the local construction workers [....]. In Barkai, the construction of the huts began immediately upon the kibbutz's founding. Seven years later, on 10/27/1956, a decision was made at the kibbutz meeting, that toilets would be erected next to each hut! The huts were initially used for residence, then a clinic, and later for the "Youth Aliya", for young people before or after their army service, and of course for volunteers. There are

no records of how many such huts were built in Barkai. Some of them crumbled over time and some were burned down.[36]

These days, more than seventy-five years after the arrival of the first Nordic wooden hut in Israel, dozens are still standing on the ground in various localities throughout Israel, among others in Be'eri, Burgata, Eilat, Ein Carmel, Ein Zurim, Gaaton, Gilad, Givat Haim (Ihud), Gvulot, Haifa, Hatzerim, Jerusalem, Kfar Achim, Kfar Masaryk, Lavi, Mashabei Sade, Naan, Nahariya, Nachsholim, Nachshonim, Nir Eliyahu, Regavim, Sde Boker, Sde Nehemiah, Tel Aviv, Tifrach, Timrat, and Yanuv.[37] Some of the wooden huts have undergone renovation and conservation procedures while others are in advanced stages of decay. Mainly in kibbutzim and moshavim, the wooden huts have become nostalgic assets over the years, and today they are often used as museums that reflect the beginnings of the settlement's history. In doing so, they bear witness not only to the challenges that the residents of kibbutzim and moshavim faced in their early years, especially the housing crisis, but also to the ideological changes that its members have undergone since those days. In 2007, a few days before the demolition of the last wooden hut in the kibbutz, the archivist of Bet Ha'Emek published "The Ballad of the Swedish Hut":

> With the establishment of the state, several hundred wooden huts made in Sweden were brought to Israel. These arrived disassembled in various packages and were erected by local workforce (mostly new immigrants). Included in the packages was also insulation material, which the people from the Jewish Agency considered unnecessary in the Israeli "hot" climate, and the buildings were erected without insulation in the walls and in the roof that was covered by local tiles. All other components were erected as provided: windows, doors, etc. The huts were not painted and remained in their original basic color. No toilets were installed in the huts and they mainly served the first residents, the pioneers, until the Jewish Agency provided permanent housing. In Bet Ha'Emek four huts were erected, meaning 16 units, where the caravans are standing today. In the 1960s, every two units were joined together, toilets were added, and a kitchenette was built at the entrance. These apartments were the first to be adapted for family accommodation: one room served as a 'living room' that included the parents' room, and the other room served the children. Over time, the families moved to permanent housing, the huts were filled with volunteers and temporary workers, the roof covering was replaced,

one building burned down, and after years of neglect, the houses were removed.[38]

In conclusion, the arrival of thousands of Nordic wooden huts in Israel in the late 1940s and early 1950s reflects the many challenges faced by the young country at that time: a frantic search for housing solutions for numerous immigrants who arrived within a limited number of years, the difficulties of their integration into the local population, the lack of private and collective economic resources, inexperienced local government, state mechanisms that rivaled over areas of responsibility, and the establishment of Israel's relations with the Diaspora (mainly through the Jewish Agency). Nordic wood huts, it seems, provided both a challenge and a solution to these problems.

NOTES

1. All data in this paragraph is taken from Moshe Lissak, *The Mass Immigration in the 1950s—the Failure of the Melting Pot Policy* (Jerusalem: Bialik Institute, 1999), pp. 3–7.
2. Y. Reiser to E. Kaplan, May 21, 1946. S14/68, Central Zionist Archives, Jerusalem.
3. Contract between the Jewish Agency and the Central Israel Trading and Investment Company Ltd. S14/40, Central Zionist Archives, Jerusalem.
4. In 1950, for example, an Amidar neighborhood was established in Acre. This neighborhood consisted of 200 wooden huts, which constituted 800 housing units. D. Rosen to the Director of the Department for Self-Government, May 15, 1950. In Dov Rosen (ed.), Ma'barot ye-yishuve 'olim: ba-aspaḳlarya shel Misrad ha-penim [Settlements and Immigration settlements: from the viewpoint of the Interior Ministry], Volume I (Jerusalem: Ha-misrad publication, 1985), p. 73.
5. L34/355, Central Zionist Archives, Jerusalem.
6. A. Shalmon to A. Nissan, October 24, 1951. L34/89, Central Zionist Archives, Jerusalem.
7. Israeli Delegation in Stockholm to the Economic Department, February 20, 1952. 1791/4-חצ, Israel State Archives, Jerusalem.
8. Israeli Consul in Helsinki to the Economic Department, June 27, 1950. 1787/1-חצ, Israel State Archives, Jerusalem.

9. Contract between the Housing Division of the Israeli Ministry of Labor and the Finnish timber company Puurakenne, April 21, 1952. 2354/7-ג, National State Archives, Jerusalem.
10. For example, A. Shalmon to A. Nissan, October 24, 1951. L34/1, Central Zionist Archives, Jerusalem.
11. Economic Department to A. Shalmon, September 19, 1951. L34/1, Central Zionist Archives, Jerusalem.
12. L. Eshkol to G. Hammer, August 29, 1952. L34/415, Central Zionist Archives, Jerusalem.
13. The Integration Department to the Ministry of the Interior—the Department for Immigrant Resettlement, April 29, 1953. In Dov Rosen (ed.), Ma'barot ye-yishuve 'olim: ba-aspaḵlarya shel Misrad ha-penim [Settlements and Immigration settlements: from the viewpoint of the Interior Ministry], Volume I (Jerusalem: Ha-misrad publication, 1985), p. 243.
14. Report of the inter-ministerial committee for the coordination of social services in the immigration settlements. Ibid., p. 157.
15. See the guarantees requested by the Jewish Agency from the Ministry of Finance. May 21, 1951. L34/355, Central Zionist Archives, Jerusalem.
16. The Finnish timber company Puurakenne to D. Givon, November 27, 1951. ג-2354/7, Israel State Archives, Jerusalem.
17. Minutes of the government's meeting, June 26, 1952. ISA-PMO-GovernmentMeeting-0002eed, Israel State Archives, Jerusalem, p. 23.
18. G. Asher to Balkin, March 16, 1952. גל-9249/4, Israel State Archives, Jerusalem.
19. F. Weinberg to the Ministry of Health, July 29, 1949. ג-2711/6, Israel State Archives, Jerusalem.
20. Letter to G. Zach in the Prime Minister's office [addressee not found], August 29, 1949. ג-2711/6, Israel State Archives, Jerusalem.
21. Cherniak to Kotler, November 30, 1949. ג-2711/6, National State Archives, Jerusalem.
22. For more, see Orna Keren-Carmel, *Israel and Scandinavia: The Beginning of Relations*, (Haifa: Pardes, 2021), pp. 57–59.
23. In an article in *Haaretz* newspaper from 2019, the topic of which was Benny Gantz—the 20th Chief of Staff and later a politician—his childhood years in moshav Kfar Achim were described. Among

other things, the article emphasized the influence of his father, Nachum Gantz, on the moshav's establishment: "Already from a young age, the father stood out in political circles. He was a member of Mapai, served as chairman of the Moshav Association, and held positions in the Jewish Agency and the Moshav Movement. Thanks to his connections, he was able to obtain a donation of several dozen wooden huts to Kfar Ahim, and he housed his family in one of them. 'For us, it was a palace,' said Gantz when he recalled his childhood." In: Hilo Glazer and Nir Gontarz, 'Gantz is often silent, but over the years he has scattered hints about his worldview. A profile.' Haaretz, February 27, 2019. https://www.haaretz.co.il/magazine/2019-02-27/ty-article-magazine/.premium/0000017f-df2a-df9c-a17f-ff3ad0800000

24. Hilde Henriksen Waage, 'Norway: One of Israel's Best Friends', *Journal of Peace Research* 37, no. 2 (2000), p. 201.
25. 'Yitzhak Allal, a survivor of the death plane in Norway, wants to be an engineer'. Maariv, September 5, 1956, p. 8 [Hebrew].
26. C. Sheba to G. Asher, March 11, 1952. 9249/4-גל, Israel State Archives, Jerusalem.
27. 'Development budget—medical buildings for the fiscal year 1950/51', August 29, 1951. 9249/4-גל, Israel State Archives, Jerusalem.
28. "Prefabricated buildings in Finland", June 18, 1951. גל-9249/4, Israel State Archives, Jerusalem.
29. G. Asher to Head of the Public Works Department, March 23, 1952. 9249/4-גל, Israel State Archives, Jerusalem.
30. C. Sheba to G. Asher, November 27, 1951. 9249/4-גל, Israel State Archives, Jerusalem.
31. G. Asher to the Minister of Health, January 21, 1952. 9249/4-גל, Israel State Archives, Jerusalem.
32. Minutes of the one hundred and thirty-eighth session of the Second Knesset, November 18, 1952, p. 93. Website of the Israeli Knesset: https://main.knesset.gov.il/activity/plenum/pages/Sessions.aspx
33. https://www.nostal.co.il/Site.asp?table=Terms&option=single&serial=3517&subject=%F0%E5
34. MAAZ (עמ"צ) Agreement, August 21, 1955. 9249/6-גל, Israel State Archives, Jerusalem.
35. Minutes of the one hundred and nine session of the Ninth Knesset, November 3, 1970, p. 28.

Website of the Israeli Knesset: https://main.knesset.gov.il/act ivity/plenum/pages/Sessions.aspx
36. Kibbutz Barkai Archive (no author): https://www.moreshet.bar kai.org.il/%D7%94%D7%A6%D7%A8%D7%99%D7%A3%D7%94% D7%A9%D7%95%D7%95%D7%93%D7%99
37. I would like to thank Ido Yinon wholeheartedly for this valuable information, which was collected in a meticulous manner, using feet and wheels.
38. Bet Ha'Emek Archive, compiled and edited by Freddy Kahana: https://www.aroundy.com/_sites/bemek/posts/ghsdTB0aRq67 YTPj/Rde8EV.pdf

CHAPTER 5

"Adolescence is a serious problem of life": N. F. S Grundtvig, Martin Buber and Adult Education in Israel

Abstract This chapter explores the close connections between the ideas of the Danish educator N.F.S. Grundtvig, the Israeli philosopher Martin Buber and the latter's establishment of 'Beit-HaMidrash Le-morei Am' (School for Educators of the People) in Jerusalem in 1949. There were similarities not only between the institutions they founded, and their educational aims, but also in the way they taught. In many ways, Grundtvig's mid-nineteenth century vision on adult education, translated by Buber, was realized a century later in Israel, a testament to the extensive transfer of ideas between Denmark and Israel unknown until now.

Keywords Martin Buber · N.F.S. Grundtvig · Denmark · Beit-Hamidrash Le-morei Am (School for Educators of the People) · Adult education · Hebrew University of Jerusalem · National identity

On January 25th, 1949, the first elections were held in the State of Israel. Two months later, Prime Minister David Ben Gurion invited to his home leading intellectuals, writers, poets and academics, and asked their opinion on the role they should play in the process of building the nation. The decisive answer of the philosopher and educator Martin Buber stood out above all: the most important role is in the spiritual absorption, and not

© The Author(s), under exclusive license to Springer Nature Switzerland AG 2024
O. Keren-Carmel, *Nordic Traces in Israel*,
https://doi.org/10.1007/978-3-031-75287-2_5

just material, of the masses of Jewish immigrants that have recently arrived and which number is about to drastically grow in the upcoming years. But how should this, according to Buber, be achieved?

> There is no other way to fulfill this role but to create a large institution for the education of the people. In the middle of the last century, during the years of the "cold and hot" war between the Germans and the Danes, a man of spirit, Sven Grundtvig, established a great enterprise for the education of the people. In this way, he and those who followed him overcame the crisis that befell the Danish people before and after the defeat, and it is amazing that the development of the enterprise and its success came after the defeat. This enterprise teaches us a great rule, which is - that the education of the people mainly depends on the close relationship between the teachers and the students (in Denmark the students were the sons of farmers and farm workers) and the essential influence of the teachers, while the main thing is not the teaching but the mental attitude, the whole being. And that is not all: the learners become the teachers, and this process keeps renewing itself ad infinitum. A dynamic ladder was created between the people of the spirit and the people.[1]

In 1949, Buber was able to accurately predict the future. With the establishment of the state there was a steep increase in the number of Jewish immigrants. Most of them did not speak the Hebrew language and did not know neither the history of the country nor its culture. The state authorities, for their part, had major difficulties fulfilling the basic needs of the immigrants in the areas of housing, employment, and health, and they often had to settle for quick and not necessarily high-quality solutions. In addition, there was a serious shortage in exactly the field that Martin Buber predicted: adult education. There were not enough teachers in Israel who could teach the new immigrants the Hebrew language and make them part of the developing Israeli society. Buber acted in a swift and practical manner: only six months after he visited Prime Minister Ben Gurion at his home, he inaugurated the Beit-Hamidrash le-morei am (School for Educators of the People) in Jerusalem.

Buber, as he mentioned, relied on a higher authority. His School for Educators of the People was based on the ideas of the Dane Nikolai Frederik Severin Grundtvig, who established the first enterprise in the world for the education of the people. This chapter deals with the educational institution founded by Martin Buber in the Talbiyeh neighborhood of Jerusalem in 1949. It reveals fascinating connections between Buber's educational teachings and that of Grundtvig, and testifies to the great influence the latter had on the former when developing the field of adult education in the newly established State of Israel. The chapter is based on documents taken from the Hebrew University archives, articles by Martin Buber and his personal letters, as well as selected writings authored by N. F. S. Grundtvig.

The Long Path to the Establishment of the School for Educators of the People

Martin Buber was born in 1878 in Vienna and died in 1965 in Jerusalem. There are many who claim that until today there is no other Israeli philosopher who left such a significant mark on the world. Despite his extensive research in the fields of religion, sociology, and literature, his influence was mainly manifested in his interpretation of contemporary issues, such as the essence of Judaism for modern Jews, Zionist nationalism, the Jewish–Arab conflict, kibbutz socialism and the meaning of man in the modern world. But above all these, argued Yaron Kalman, a researcher and a student of Buber, he was an adult educator.[2]

The opening in Jerusalem of Buber's School for Educators of the People in 1949 was the culmination of a long process that began half a century earlier. Over the years, although the reasons and circumstances surrounding the vision of the school have changed frequently, its core remained the same. It was in 1901, at the age of 23, that Buber proposed for the first time to establish a Jewish university in Jerusalem.[3] A year later, together with Berthold Feibel and Chaim Weizmann, the proposal became a concrete plan, and they published the booklet "Jewish High School" in which Jewish youth, mainly from Eastern European countries, could "develop their spiritual powers—the powers of the nation—in freedom and far from any kind of discrimination."[4] The reason why the three authors conceived the idea of establishing a Jewish high school was directly related to the difficulties at that time of Jewish youth to be admitted to academic institutions and to develop their skills, mainly due to the *numerus clausus*—the limitation imposed on the number of Jewish students who were allowed to study at universities. The connection between adult education and national identity was already clear to the authors at that time:

And the high school, by its very essence, is most tightly connected to the great national freedom movement. A Jewish high school in itself will already be a visible sign of the living Jewish nationhood, of the creative Jewish spirit: in the eyes of those who oblige the existence of the people of Israel and its future and life – it will be their spiritual center; those who doubt the Jewish people - will have a new and powerful source; and against those who seek to kill the Jewish people or cause their salvation – it will serve as an undestroyable fortress.[5]

This booklet was the first theoretical program for the establishment of the Hebrew University in Jerusalem.[6] However, a more detailed and mature proposal of the plan was submitted by Buber in 1924, during the actual planning of the university, which lasted about seven years— from the laying of the cornerstone in July 1918 to the inauguration of the university in April 1925. The school Buber proposed was supposed to be part of the Hebrew University in Jerusalem, to be called Volkshochschule (an exact translation of Grundtvig's Folkhøjskole), and not to be regarded as a university branch but as an independent institute that links the university and the people. This is how Buber envisioned the planned school:

Young people (who in my mind are between the ages of 16 and 25) do interchangeably spiritual and physical work (especially garden work) and play for six months, together with their teachers in the village, and it should not be overlooked that the meals and the social events are also largely part of the institution's work. And it becomes clear, that the essence of an institution such as this is reflected in a simple conversation in the middle of a day, when it unwittingly and unintentionally expands into space and depth and becomes a pure and true learning, the spirit of which does not come from the purpose of teaching and learning, but for the sake of seeking the truth and finding it together, until the rabbi's [teacher's – O.K.C] bewilderment is not less than the student's. And even more you feel the bustle and activity while in the evening everyone is sitting together at the edge of the forest in silence, and in this silence, there is a being and a security that nobody can wordily express.[7]

The board of trustees of the Hebrew University enthusiastically accepted Buber's proposal. Nevertheless, plans and reality collided. Before Buber had the chance to immigrate to Palestine and fulfill his vision, circumstances gave rise to a new, even more urgent need for the establishment of a Jewish institution for adult education. And not in

Jerusalem—but in Germany. In 1933 Buber founded the Center for Jewish Adult Education (Mittelstelle für jüdische Erwachsenbildung), which was designed to provide a response to the many challenges of German Jews after the rise to power of the National Socialist Party. The purpose of the institution was to strengthen, through spiritual resistance, the self-awareness of the Jews as individuals and as a group. Yaron Kalman, Buber's student, claimed that Buber's greatest educational influence was manifested in this institution, of which he stood at the head until 1938 when he immigrated to Palestine.[8]

It took eleven more years, before Buber finally established the School for Educators of the People in Jerusalem—the educational institution that he envisioned about half a century earlier. Although it is easy to identify the spirit of the Jewish High School that Buber conceived in 1901 within the School for Educators of the People which he founded in 1949, the completely different historical circumstances that occurred by then led to far-reaching changes in his initial plan.

Buber intended in 1901 to cultivate a new Jewish figure. One that can develop and be educated according to its natural abilities, that can resist tyrannical forces through inner resilience, and that will be a driving force in the rebuilding of the Jewish people in the Land of Israel, without losing his unique individual and cosmopolitan values. The intended educational enterprise was supposed to provide the students with a broad Jewish identity, which would help them to deal with the complex and frequently changing reality. Yet, in accordance with the new circumstances that have arisen, the School for the Educators of the People in 1949 was required to educate teachers who will focus, first and foremost, on the teaching of the Hebrew language to adult immigrants and thus in fact enable them to integrate as quickly as possible into the work environment of the young country. As a result of the close connection between the establishment of the school and the mass immigration, the fate of the former was also decided: in 1954, when the immigration waves dwindled and narrowed, the school was closed. The flagship of adult education in Israel, as Buber conceived and planned for fifty years, closed down with a whimper.

THE SCHOOL FOR EDUCATORS OF THE PEOPLE

In 1951, Buber published another booklet called "The School for Educators of the People—Its Purpose and Plan" published by the Center for the Education of the People in Jerusalem,[9] in which he explained the two main goals for which the school was founded. The first was the spiritual-cultural absorption of the great waves of immigration that arrived in Israel at that time, and the second was the education of the people, i.e. the education of a person for intellectual independence through the development of his existing qualities and talents. The two goals, according to Buber, coalesce together in the School for Educators of the People. The study of the Hebrew language, which was a tool used daily by the immigrants, was taught in the school as an end in itself—in order to capture the Israeli people, teach their culture, and renew the language according to the new reality of the present. The Hebrew language, Buber claimed, was a gateway to the rich and ancient world called the culture of Israel.

The study program in the school was divided into three clusters. The first included the study of the Hebrew language, the Bible, the history of the people of Israel, and the knowledge of the land. To complete, Jewish studies such as Mishnah, Folklore, Jewish philosophy, Kabbalah, and Hebrew literature were also taught. The second cluster dealt with pedagogical training: studying the principles of education, didactics, and the teaching of the Bible for adults. As part of it, the students were teaching in immigrant camps (Ma'abarot) to get practical work experience. The third cluster was aimed at general education, and taught the basics of philosophical thought, general history, economics, the history of the Arab people, state and society, natural sciences (biology, genetics, atomic theory and cosmology), art and public singing. Renowned scholars from a variety of fields taught at the School, including Yehoshua Leibovitch, Gershom Sholem, Ernst Simon, Hugo Bergman, Nathan Rottenstreich, and of course Martin Buber. The students studied an average of 32 hours a week, and the rest of the study was done in groups or individually—according to the student's wishes.

During its years of activity, the School suffered from three main difficulties. The first difficulty was financial. The joint funding of the School by a number of different agents led to an attempt by each financier to reduce his share. Even after it was closed, the school was still in debt to the Hebrew University, the Center for the Education of the People, the teachers of the school, and the administrators of the school (the couple Gideon and Hadassah Freudenberg). The vast majority of its financial problems were resolved on March 12, 1954, about six months after it closed its doors, when the third Minister of Education and Culture Ben-Zion Dinur signed a written commitment to cover, retrospectively, the school's budget.

The second difficulty was more fundamental, and concerned the degree of independence of the school as an educational institution. Although the school arose out of the Center for the Education of the People at the Hebrew University, which also provided it with secretarial and library services, Buber strove to maintain the school as a completely separate institution both conceptually and structurally. Furthermore, Buber refused to allow the Center for the Education of the People to approve or reject appointments of teachers to the School. This decision, he argued, should remain with the management of the school only. In the Center for the Education of the People it was argued, on the other hand, that being the one that pays the teachers' salaries, the center should also be the one who appoints them. After stormy discussions in the meetings of the school's executive committee, decisions were made on both issues against Buber's opinion: it was determined that the school would be an institution **of** the university and not **near** the university, and that the Center for the Education of the People would be the body responsible of approving the appointments of teachers at the school.[10]

However, the question of the school's independence did not end there. The Israeli government (through the Ministry of Education and Culture) and the Jewish Agency were the main financiers of the school, since its stated goal was to enable the country to absorb waves of immigrants—a task of the state. However, the premise of both the management of the Center for the Education of the People at the Hebrew University and that of the school was that it must remain completely independent in its activities and that the state should not be allowed to have any influence on the content taught or the staffing of the teachers. Indeed, the decision was made that the board of the school would consist of three representatives of the university, one representative of the government, and one representative of the Jewish agency, so that an automatic majority would be created for the university over the government and the Jewish a-Agency.[11]

The last difficulty was related to the disputes that arose between the members of the executive committee of the school regarding the place of Jewish studies within the curriculum.[12] Buber claimed, rather surprisingly, that the study of Jewish history should be completely omitted from the curriculum of the school, while the other members strongly opposed it. The first Minister of Education and Culture, Zalman Shazar, argued that the curriculum should include a series of lectures on prominent Jewish movements and figures in history; the chairman of the Jewish Agency, Berl Locker, argued that the focus should be on studying the history of the Israeli diaspora in modern times; and the chairman of the committee, Prof. Simcha Assaf, requested the studies will focus on at least one period in the history of Israel—such as the Second Temple or modern times. At the end of the meeting, a joint decision was made, according to which the curriculum of the school should be expanded to include the history of Israel as well.

The first study cycle at the school opened on December 4, 1949 and ended on October 25, 1950. Of the 43 enrolled students, 12 were new immigrants (from Morocco, Tunisia, Turkey, Romania, Poland, France, England, and Argentina) and the rest were born in Palestine. 30 teachers participated in the teaching in the first cycle. About half of the students, 22 in number, lived in boarding conditions inside the school. After a practical work at the Beit-Lid immigrant camp during the summer months, 36 of the students successfully completed the school year, and were accepted immediately to various teaching positions throughout the country. Three more cohorts of students were qualified at the school, until it closed at the end of its fourth academic year, on June 2, 1953. Then the Department of Adult Education at the School of Education at the Hebrew University received the school building in Talbiyeh and continued to engage in adult education.

Grundtvigian Inspiration

N.F.S. Grundtvig (1783–1872) is considered the most influential Dane ever to have lived. He was a historian, preacher, politician, theologian, and poet. Over his lifetime, he wrote more than 1500 patriotic hymns that were part of his lifelong struggle to define and preserve Danish culture in the face of strong influences from southern neighbor Germany. He also became the founding father of the folk high school. This new kind of school was aimed for young adults, in order both to educate the individual and to strengthen the national Danish spirit. In Grundtvig's words, its main objective was not to enrich the students with academic knowledge but to enlighten human life.

The similarity between Buber's School for Educators of the People and Grundtvig's folk high school is obvious from the first glance. It is evident not only in the conceptual structure of the two institutions but also, and perhaps mainly, in the manner in which the studies were conducted. With a difference of about a century, the two institutions founded by Grundtvig and Buber tried to meet similar needs in a similar way, if also under completely different external circumstances. The great similarity between them can be found in three main areas: teacher-student relations, the relationship between adult education and the shaping of national identity, and adult education as a response to extreme times.

TEACHER-STUDENT RELATIONS

In his essay *The School for Life* (published in English in 2011 by Aarhus University Press), Grundtvig stated that the foundation of his folk high schools would not be books, authorities or the duty to transmit knowledge, but rather meetings, conversations and exchanges of ideas between the educator and the students. With this approach, Grundtvig came out against the schools in Denmark at the time, which focused on the study of science, language, industry and commerce, and were intended to educate the sons of the rising bourgeois class. Grundtvig's folk high schools focused on the landscape, nature, law, and the Danish nation and advocated a joint education of the peasantry and the bourgeoisie. His educational approach was, therefore, based on participation—in the life of the people, equality between the classes, and the "living word"—emphasis on dialogue and not on memorizing texts.[13] In the middle of the nineteenth century, this educational approach was no less than revolutionary, and the emphasis on the "living word" was its main innovation:

> The "living word", i.e. the spoken word, was to Grundtvig the highest medium for expressing personality and, therefore, to him the most potent force in education. [...] [I]t maintains the personal contact between teacher and pupil and between one pupil and another that is the core of the Grundtvig system. It is, indeed, this contact that helps to fuse the heterogeneous group into a living fellowship.[14]

Martin Buber, similarly to Grundtvig, particularly emphasized the importance of the relationship between the educator and his students. In 1919, he gave a lecture entitled "On the educational act" (Rede über das Erzieherische) in Heppenheim, Germany, where he presented the educational act as a dialogue, an idea that over the years became the basis of his well-known "dialogic principle in education." This principle focused on the relationship that is created between the being of the educator and the being of the student and on the personal relationship that develops between them. Education must be conducted as a dialogue in which both parties share a partnership of truth, especially when it comes to educating adults. Their conversation must

> be based on questions from both sides, and not on questions that the student asks from below and the teacher answers from above, from the chair to the benches, but on mutual questions. And it does not only concern Socratic questions - but real questions that trouble the ones who ask them and for which they have no answer, and the students' answers will give them, the teachers themselves, the knowledge they lack - the knowledge of their students' experience. [...] This thesis puts in front of the authoritative teacher, who knows the answers, a figure of an educator who does not have a message, and who asks questions; In Buber's words, as he testifies himself, "I have nothing to teach - I am having a conversation".[15]

Both Grundtvig and Buber saw the relationship between the student and the educator as the core of the educational act. Both tried to reduce the built-in distance between them and increase the feeling of mutual identification through an emphasis on the mental connection that develops between the participants in an educational act.

In this context, Buber extensively mentioned Grundtvig's student, Christen Kold, who in his opinion embodied the character of the ultimate educator, in that he did not believe in the sustenance of the brain alone but cared for the development of the whole person: it was desirable that the student learn to think, "but not only with his mind, but with all his spiritual-physical being, with all his organs and senses."[16] The person responsible for this way of learning, according to Buber, is the educator. Thus, Buber's "dialogic principle" and Grundtvig's "living word" both express the exact same approach: it is the verbal and interpersonal relationship between the educator and the student that stand at the basis of the educational act, nothing else.

Emphasizing the mental well-being of the student during the educational act led them both to another common conclusion: the importance of the relationship between the students and themselves. The contribution of an educator to the educational act is not enough, the support of the study group is also required. This understanding led Buber and Grundtvig (and especially his student Christen Kold) to hold a significant part of the studies in the form of group learning, in fellowship. In his descriptions of his school, Buber reiterated that most of the study hours are not held in the frontal teaching method, but in study groups. This is also the case in the Danish folk high schools, which to this day operate in accordance with the approach that the highest educational value is obtained in group learning.

The importance they saw in the learning group led them to another understanding, namely that it is appropriate to spend the study period in boarding school conditions. Christen Kold, for example, lived together with his students in the folk high school that he founded in Ryslinge in 1851. In Buber's school, where about half of the students lived in boarding school conditions, the principal of the school Gideon Freudenberg and his wife Hadassah lived both with them. The large amount of time that the students and their educators spent in each other's company, their shared challenges and activities, made the study period, both in Denmark and in Israel, a unique experience.

Adult Education and National Identity

The second similarity between Grundtvig and Buber lied in the connecting thread they identified between adult education and the shaping of national identity. Buber saw the mass immigration to Israel as the greatest challenge to the construction of the young country's national identity. In a very short time, people from different countries, different continents, and different ethnicities arrived in Israel, which made it difficult for the nation to develop a uniform culture based on common traditions. The only way to do this, according to Buber, was through adult education: by returning to the eternal values of the national heritage and through a search for their meeting points with everyday life and reality. Buber, in many ways, saw his role in contributing to the creation of a new Israeli Jew. But how will it be conducted practically?

> The Hebrew language must be taught not only for its own sake, but also as the bearer of our share in eternal values; the Bible must be taught not only as the supreme asset of our national culture, but also as part of the people of Israel in the eternal values; and the same is the case with the history of Israel, in which it is not enough to reveal the path of the nation through the spans of time, but one must delve into its meaning, which is the great masterpiece that testifies to this people, who went around proclaiming the values of justice and peace not because they were weak, but because they were loyal to these values; and even the knowledge of the land must be taught as a basis for the same promise to humanity that is involved in this land. In the same words, the students must be instructed about the reality

of life, but their eyes and hearts must be opened to see that it is also a tool for the truth of the spirit and its way in the world.[17]

At the same time, Buber believed that in order to understand the reality in which he lives, the adult must not only be part of the community, learn to understand it, identify with it and live within it, but also have an individual identity, an understanding of his unique place within the community. Accordingly, a person is not allowed to abandon his own values and moral principles just in order to adapt to the environment in which he lives, and he is also not allowed to ignore his environment and live only according to his own desires and needs. In this, Buber saw the basis for adult education: the preservation of a personal identity while adapting it to the collective identity of the community.

However, the close connection between adult education and the strengthening of a contemporary national identity was recognized not only by Buber; a century earlier Grundtvig also recognized it. Grundtvig considered the study of reality itself, life as it is, the main educational content. Thus, the studies of the past as expressed in the New Testament and Norse mythology, not only lead to a gradual understanding of the meaning of life, and in this way they reveal the inner values of the people, but also symbolically present the way in which the ancestors dealt with essential issues of human existence.[18] In accordance,

> Students at the folk high school should not be made passive, analytical observers of history, but active participants who themselves could create history. The past should be the basis of the present, and the teaching of it not dry, but living, poetic.[19]

Buber, as well, saw in Bible studies, Hassidism (his research expertise) and legends as the basis for Hebrew humanism, which he wanted to instill in his students as the basis for a new personal and national identity:

> [D]espite Buber's extensive philosophical and historical knowledge, his educational ideology was that knowledge is not the final aim of education, but a means to help clarify values and a proper way of living. He regarded his literary adaptations of the texts he chose from Hasidic literature as a way of winning over the audience, and as a means to arouse discussion of the existential meaning the stories elicited.[20]

This approach, of course, was not unique to Grundtvig and Buber, it was part of a broader international perception that reached its peak during the 1950s, 1960s, and 1970s, when schools for adults were established in many parts of the world, especially in developing countries that gained independence in those years. Educational enterprises in the form of Grundtvig's folk high schools, which focused on turning adults into conscious and productive citizens, were used to strengthen national identity among the inhabitants of the young countries that arose following the decolonization process. Grundtvig and Buber, like many others, saw the study of past events as a means of shaping the present. They believed that history allows the adult to get to know himself and at the same time also the country and the reality in which he lives in a deeper way; to learn from the accumulated life experience of the ancient ancestors of the nation and at the same time create a sense of belonging and identification with the national community.

ADULT EDUCATION AS RESPONSE TO EXTREME SITUATIONS

The third point of similarity between Grundtvig's and Buber's educational approach is expressed in their view that adult education can provide an adequate response, even if partial, to situations of national crisis. In 1927, a German translation of a selection of Grundtvig's writings was published for the first time. The translator, Johannes Tiedje, grew up as part of the German minority in Schleswig–Holstein in the shadow of the struggles between Germany (led by Prussia) and Denmark over it. Tiedje experienced firsthand the changes that took place following the First Schleswig War (1848–1851), when the area became part of Denmark, as well as the Prussian and Austrian victory in the Second Schleswig War (1864), following which the area became German again. At the time of the publication of Tiedje's translation of Grundtvig's writings, the northern region of Schleswig returned to Danish control following a referendum held there in 1920. In the introduction to the book he translated, Tiedje described his feelings as a teenager following the self-initiated secession of his Danish friends from him and from other German teenagers due to the tension created between the Danish majority and the German minority toward the end of the nineteenth century. Its origin, so he claimed, was Grundtvig's unprecedented influence on shaping the new identity of the Danish youth. Grundtvig was the one who tore his friends from him, taught them new Danish songs, new dances, and preached in churches sermons that the Germans did not understand. In a short time, his Danish friends became entirely different people:

> Wir sahen unsere Kameraden ein schllichtes gerades Leben führen, sie wurden unter der Hand dieses Zauberers Grundtvig zu besseren und tüchtigeren Menschen, die ihres bäuerlichen Standes bescheiden froh, geistige Güter und Ziele in freier Anneigung gewannen.[21]
> [We have seen our friends leading simple and honest lives; Under the hands of this wizard Grundtvig they became better and more capable people, who - modestly happy with their peasant status - won a free spirit and financial reward. My translation – O.K.C.]

Martin Buber, as well, lived and worked in turbulent times. The Center for Jewish Adult Education that he founded in Germany in 1933 arose from the renewed need for Jewish education and Jewish culture following the fall of the Weimar Republic and the rise of the German National Socialist Party to power. The studies at this center were intended for adults and did not focus on imparting knowledge, but on making learning the basis of Jewish identity, as a means of "surviving the storm" that German Jews found themselves in.[22] Sixteen years later, in 1949, Buber identified another situation of national crisis,[23] this time in the form of the waves of mass immigration that reached the young Israeli state and the urgency of finding solutions for their proper spiritual absorption. Since Buber believed that the adult is only able to change in times of crisis, when he is required to mobilize all the forces inherent in him to deal with the new situation,[24] he therefore decided to establish in Jerusalem the School for Educators of the people.

Implicit and Explicit Inspiration

The first time that Buber was able to read, in the German language, about Grundtvig's original educational approach was in Johannes Tiedje's previously mentioned book, which was published in Jena in 1927, and which presented Grundtvig's writings on the folk high schools. This was about the time when Buber submitted his detailed plan for the establishment of the Center for Adult Education at the Hebrew University of Jerusalem. But Buber had heard of Grundtvig and had known of his educational approach for quite a few years before that. Already in 1919,

Buber delivered a lecture in the city of Heppenheim, in a conference aimed to renew the education system in Germany. In the conference he argued that a university should fulfill two needs at the same time: research institutes whose purpose is to fulfill the needs of scientific research and professional training, and alongside them a high school that provides education to the nation and contributes to the building of its spiritual life. The high school, so claimed Buber, should be organizationally similar to Grundtvig's folk high school and should also be influenced by the Dane's teaching methods.[25]

Despite this, over the years, Buber rarely referred to Grundtvig and his considerable influence on his own educational concept. In fact, in his many publications in the field of education in general and in adult education specifically, Buber mentioned Grundtvig's name only twice. The first time was as part of a lecture he delivered during the 21st conference of the German Zionists, in 1926 (it was later published under the name "Education of the People—Our Role"). Grundtvig was mentioned there only in one sentence:

> As centers for the education of the people, as I see them, I imagine some kind of dormitories, which in the Land of Israel will merge with urban and other courses and will become a central school for the education of the people, whose form is the same for the whole country; whereas in the Diaspora, wherever they can be established, they will usually be each for itself. And in this, I see in front of my eyes the rural schools for the education of the people that were founded in the middle of the 19th century by the great Danish patriot Grundtvig.[26]

The folk high schools that Grundtvig founded were used here by Buber as an example of centers for the education of the people that should be adopted by the Zionist movement. Buber saw them as crossroads in the form of institutions whose purpose was to link one generation to the next one, and thus generate the new home of a new Jewish humanity.

The second and last time that Buber mentioned Grundtvig's name in his publications occurred twenty-four years later, in an article titled "Adult Education" that was published in *Molad* journal in 1950.[27] The article was written and published at the very time when the doors of Buber's School for Educators of the People in Jerusalem opened for the first time, and apparently it was intended, at least in part, to offer a comprehensive explanation for its establishment—to lead adult immigrants to spiritual independence while uniting them as a people. In the article, Buber clearly stated the obvious similarity between his own approach and that of Grundtvig as well as his student Christen Kold, in regard to the nature of the learning process. In this, Buber concluded, "the principle laid down at the foundation of Grundtvig's method, which I call the dialogic principle in education, is embodied."[28] It is possible that Buber's choice to mention Grundtvig, his student Christen Kold and the folk high schools that they established, for the first time in an extensive and detailed manner, was due to the need to anchor the new educational institution he founded at the time in a successful historical example.

Contrary to Buber himself, who claimed that his "dialogical principle" did not stem from any external influence but was the result of personal inspiration, a vision that accompanied him since his youth,[29] quite a few researchers who dealt with Buber's educational approach recognized and described the considerable similarity between his approach and that of Grundtvig's "living word." For example, Morgan and Guilherme stated that "Grundtvig's influence on Buber continued throughout his life, and was one of the driving forces."[30] Also Pauker and Klieger: "In Israel, during the 1950s, Martin Buber acknowledged Grundtvig's approach and founded a school for community teachers."[31] Or in the context of the establishment of the educational institution Ulpan Akiva: "When Shulamit Katznelson [head of the Ulpan Akiva—O.K.C] visited the Nordic folkhighschools she was acquainted with Grundtvig's view of human nature and educational ideas which in many ways could be compared with Martin Buber's ideas and thoughts."[32] Even nowadays, a recent study program *The Community Teachers Program* (CTP), established as a collaboration between Beit Berl College and Dror Israel Movement, is declared to be based on Martin Buber's dialogical philosophy that reflects the nineteenth-century Grundtvig's idea of "community teachers." Beyond identifying the obvious similarity between Buber and Grundtvig, the above examples provide another insight: wherever Grundtvig is mentioned, he is always mentioned through Buber. It seems that in Israel, Grundtvig still does not have an independent existence as an educational figure but only as a source of inspiration for the educational enterprise of Martin Buber.[33]

Concludingly, the founding of the School for Educators of the People in 1949 by Martin Buber indicates that the transfer of ideas between Israel and Denmark is more extensive than was previously known. At the end of Buber's above-mentioned visit to David Ben Gurion in March 1949, he summarized his opinion on Israel's future challenges in the following words:

> It is true that our historical situation is radically different from the situation of the Danes in the days of Grundtvig. It is our hour of victory and not that of defeat. But I am afraid, because our crisis may come from the victory. The internal crisis is imminent, in my opinion, and the order of the hour for us is to help face it. I do not underestimate the important roles in the field of economy, politics and security, but the greatest of all roles and also the most difficult of all is the role of true absorption. What we have to do will certainly not be similar to Grundtvig's enterprise, it should be appropriate for our challenges and our needs, it should be appropriate for the human material that came to us and will come to us, human material that, according to its nature and condition, has no equal in the world.[34]

It is hard to argue, after more than seven decades since the establishment of Israel, that Buber did not predict with incredible accuracy both the challenges of his present time and the failures of the future.

Notes

1. *A Land of Two Peoples*, Martin Buber, Schocken Publishing House, Tel Aviv, 1988, p. 202. [Hebrew].
2. See Yaron Kalman, "Martin Buber (1878–1965)", *Prospects: The Quarterly Review of Comparative Education*, XXIII, no. 1/2, (1993), pp. 135–146.
3. A lecture Buber held in Vienna, published in p. 423, "On the future of the University", *Mordechai Martin Buber: Am ve'olam*, vol. 2, The Zionist Library near the Zionist Histadrut, Jerusalem, 1964. [Hebrew]
4. *Jewish High School*, Martin Buber, Berthold Feibel, Chaim Weizmann, Magnes Publishing House, Jerusalem, 1968, p. 15. [Hebrew]
5. Ibid., p. 19.
6. Ibid. introduction by Hugo Bergman, second page.
7. "Education of the People—our Role" *Mordechai Martin Buber: Am ve'olam*, vol. 2, The Zionist Library near the Zionist Histadrut, Jerusalem, 1964, p. 364. [Hebrew]

8. Yaron Kalman, "Martin Buber (1878–1965)", *Prospects: The Quarterly Review of Comparative Education*, XXIII, no. 1/2, (1993), pp. 7–8, 135–146.
9. A copy of the pamphlet is found in "Martin Buber" file, vol. IV, Hebrew University Archives.
10. Meeting of the board of directors of the Center for the education of the people at the Hebrew University, July 8, 1949. File no. 2850, Hebrew University Archives.
11. Ibid.
12. Meeting of the board of directors of the Center for the education of the people at the Hebrew University, September 26, 1949. File no. 2850, Hebrew University Archives.
13. "The Question of Dialogue in Danish: Representations of Argumentation in Curricula and Textbooks from the Perspectives of Isocrates, Grundtvig and Kierkegaard", Christina Matthiesen, in *Exploring Textbooks and Cultural Change in Nordic Education, 1536–2020*, ed. Merethe Roos (Leiden; Boston: Brill Sense, 2021), p. 358.
14. *Living Democracy in Denmark*, Peter Manniche, Publisher: Frederick A. Praeger, Inc., New York, 1952, p. 144.
15. *Sefer Shahar Studies in Adult Education*, ed. Shlomo Kadosh and Yaron Kalman, published by the Martin Buber Institute for Adult Education, Jerusalem, 1984, p. 67. [Hebrew].
16. "Adult Education", *Mordechai Martin Buber: Am ve'olam*, The Zionist Library near the Zionist Histadrut, Jerusalem, 1964, p. 402. [Hebrew].
17. Ibid., p. 408.
18. "The International Dissemination of Grundtvig's Educational Ideas", K. E. Bugge, *Grundtvig-Studier* 63, no. 1, pp. 168–177.
19. *Living Democracy in Denmark*, Peter Manniche, Publisher: Frederick A. Praeger, Inc., New York, 1952, p. 104.
20. "Jewish Nationalism as Religiosity without Religion—The Meaning of Judaism to Martin Buber and the Role of Education in Presenting this View to the Public", Ron Margolin, *Adult Education in Israel*, N. 15, 2017, pp. 150–163.
21. *N. F. S. Grundtvig, Volkheit*, translation and forwarded by Johannes Tiedje, Eugen Diedrich Verlag, Jena, 1927, p. X (Einleitung).

22. "Arming for Survival: Martin Buber and Jewish Adult Education in Nazi Germany", Yehoyakim Cochavi, *Holocaust and Genocide Studies* 3, no. 1 (1988), pp. 55–67.
23. Martin Buber saw the contribution of Grundtvig's folk high schools also in the Danish resistance during the Second World War. Already during the war, in 1940, Danish Professor of Theology Hal Koch (1904–1963) delivered surprisingly successful lectures to the general public in Denmark, which dealt with the fundamental values of Danish society, such as democracy and humanism, and the attempts of the German occupation to undermine them. Koch used the writings of Grundtvig (the object of his academic research) in his lectures, emphasizing the latter's thoughts in the field of internal cohesion, the cultivation of education, and the importance of the Danish language and Danish culture. Koch's practical political conclusion, however, was to carefully obey the unity government that ruled Denmark at the time, which advocated cooperation with the Germans, and the avoidance of any acts of resistance against them. The strength of the Danes, according to Koch, was in unity, not division. Contrary to Buber's version, then, Grundtvig's folk high schools served as a source of strengthening the cohesion of the Danish national identity, and not as a source of active resistance to the German occupation.
24. *Sefer Shahar Studies in Adult Education*, ed. Shlomo Kadosh and Yaron Kalman, published by the Martin Buber Institute for Adult Education, Jerusalem, 1984, p. 66. [Hebrew]
25. Letter no. 50, Martin Buber to Shmuel Hugo Bergman, Heppenheim, 6 January, 1920, p. 55. "Mordechai Martin Buber—letters exchange", vol. 2, 1918–1938, Yehoshua Amir and Miriam Ron, Bialik Institute, Jerusalem, 1990. [Hebrew]. And also the next letter: pp. 56–7, letter 51, Martin Buber to Shmuel Hugo Bergman, 24 January 1920.
26. "Education of the People—our Role" *Mordechai Martin Buber: Am ve'olam*, vol. 2, The Zionist Library near the Zionist Histadrut, Jerusalem, 1964, p. 363. [Hebrew]
27. *Molad*, vol. 4, February–March 1950, pp. 297–303.
28. Ibid., p. 401.
29. *Martin Buber*, Zohar Maor, Zalman Shazar Center, Jerusalem, 2016, p. 91. [Hebrew]

30. "Buber and the Holocaust", in *Buber and Education, Dialogue as Conflict Resolution*, W. John Morgan and Alexandre Guilherme, Routledge, Oxon and New York, 2014, p. 76.
31. "A Collaboration of Three Organizations: Adjusting the Professional Development School Model to Prepare Community Teachers", Alon Pauker and Aviva Klieger, in *Building and maintaining collaborative communities*, eds. Judith J. Slater, Ruth Ravid & Martin Reardon (Information Age Publishing, Charlotte NC, 2016), p. 22.
32. *Grundtvig's Educational Ideas in Japan, the Philippines and Israel*, Lilian Zollner, 1994, p. 217.
33. Surprisingly, the phenomenon of suppressing (and sometimes ignoring) Grundtvig's contribution to the field of (adult) education is not unique to Israel. It can also be found in the USA and in Canada. See for example the chapter by Clay Warren: "The International Reception of N. F. S. Grundtvig's Educational Ideas", in *The School for Life*, (Aarhus University Press, 2011), pp. 352–369.
34. *A Land of Two Peoples*, Martin Buber, Schocken Publishing House, Tel Aviv, 1988, p. 202. [Hebrew]

CHAPTER 6

Common Values, Different Interests: Early Israeli-Swedish Cooperation on Development Aid to Africa

Abstract Since its establishment in 1961 the Mount Carmel Training Centre (called today 'the Golda Meir Mashav international training Center'), located in Haifa, Israel, has had a significant as well as unique role as a bridge to North–South relations. This chapter focuses, however, on a widely neglected role of the center, namely its contribution to the development of Israeli-Swedish bilateral relations. The success of the joint venture derived not only from the fact that Israel and Sweden acted upon similar socialist values at the time, but also that both greatly benefitted from it: the young Israeli state, lacking in financial resources and not least in international allies, enjoyed a Swedish substantial budget supplement and the constructive rapprochement between the countries that followed; while Sweden, joining rather late the race of developed countries to the recently established African states, enjoyed Israel's pioneering experience in the field of development aid. Thus, the article presents the winding ways that knowledge circulated within the dominant social democratic mid-twentieth century sphere of influence.

This chapter is based on my article published in *Middle Eastern Studies*, vol. 59, no. 6 (2023), pp. 968–982. I would like to thank the editors of the journal for the permission to publish it here.

© The Author(s), under exclusive license to Springer Nature Switzerland AG 2024
O. Keren-Carmel, *Nordic Traces in Israel*,
https://doi.org/10.1007/978-3-031-75287-2_6

Keywords Sweden · Development aid · Africa · Mount Carmel Training Center (MCTC) · Community development · International Socialist · International cooperation

Since 1961, a cozy yet spacious house in Haifa, Israel, has been home to the Mount Carmel Training Center (MCTC, renamed the Golda Meir International Training Center in 1985). In spite of its relative anonymity, its importance to Israeli modern history is almost without precedence. MCTC had a uniquely significant role in various national and international events throughout the second half of the twentieth century: it became a platform for initiating and formulating Israel's provision of development aid to Africa, Asia, and Latin America; a bridge in the emerging relations between the North and the South; a base for global cooperation with international organizations, particularly the United Nations (UN) with its various institutions; and finally, a pivotal institution for the pursuit of Israeli foreign interests.

This chapter, however, focuses on a lesser-known but no less important role played by MCTC, namely, the center's contribution to the development of bilateral relations between Sweden and Israel. A review of MCTC's close cooperation with Swedish voluntary organizations and, later, state authorities reveals the intriguing relationship between the two countries, which was largely based on similar contemporary social democratic values and policies, among others in the spheres of development aid, the advancement of women, the labor movement, international organizations, and last but not least, the personal connections that have formed between officials from both countries over the years.

The chapter makes use of newly available documents on MCTC, which reveal the center's essential role within Israel's emerging foreign affairs, in relation to both the developing countries in Africa and the developed Nordic countries, in particular Sweden. These documents originate first and foremost from MCTC's Archives, supplemented by various sources from the Lavon Institute for Labor Research, the Israel State Archives, the Central Zionist Archives, the Swedish National Archives, and the Swedish International Development Cooperation Agency (SIDA) Archives.

It opens with a description of the Mount Carmel Training Center, situating it within a larger geographical, historical, and political context. The focus then narrows to Swedish-Israeli cooperation on MCTC and its origins, reasons, and various modes of operation are examined. In the last two sections, the unique characteristics of this cooperation, and the process that led to its termination, are analyzed. Finally, the conclusion aims to interweave all the previous sections, thus presenting a more nuanced understanding of Swedish-Israeli relations during the 1960s and 1970s.

Mount Carmel Training Center

The Mount Carmel Training Center was established with the aim of providing education and training in skills that would help women of developing countries make an effective contribution to their societies. The center's activities were designed to train mid-level personnel who play a vital role in promoting and expanding community development. Its premise was that the community development worker should not impose solutions from above but, rather, strive to work with the people in seeking their own solution to their problems. The center's program of activities usually covered only the coming year, and its planning did not follow pre-ordinated lines. This approach corresponded with the growing realization that program planning should be suited to the changing needs, requirements, and attitudes of the recipients of assistance, and thus had to be re-evaluated annually. The varying needs of the developing countries were continually re-examined on the basis of opinions and follow-ups provided by experts working in the developing countries, the center's annual seminar for leaders, and surveys conducted by the UN's specialized agencies.

Between 1961, the year of MCTC's establishment, and 1979, the year Sweden decided to cease funding MCTC—the two decades on which this chapter focuses—the center's program included courses of four to six months duration, study tours for groups and individuals, and leaders' seminars. All the participants from developing countries had received scholarships from one of the following sources: the Israel Association for International Cooperation (MASHAV, also known today as Israel's Agency for International Development Cooperation), the Swedish Fund at UNESCO (a special fund financed by the Swedish government within the framework of the Swedish Technical Assistance Program and administered by the United Nations Educational, Scientific and Cultural Organization, UNESCO), international women's organizations through their national affiliates, and UN specialized agencies such as FAO (Food and Agriculture Organization), UNICEF (United Nations Children's Fund), and WHO (World Health Organization). In each course the students received instruction in community development as well as one particular skill such as adult education, teaching in kindergartens and nurseries, consumer education, food and applied nutrition, handicrafts for home industries, or cooperative marketing. Throughout the courses, the lectures were followed by observation tours to institutions that engaged in the subjects taught, where the students had an opportunity to observe and discuss Israel's approach to resolving certain problems. They were then asked to evaluate these solutions in light of the conditions and resources in their own countries.

MCTC also hosted various international events during these two decades. For example, in 1964 the International Council of Social Democratic Women had its annual study-week there; that same year the Histadrut (Israel's General Federation of Labor), in cooperation with UNESCO, hosted its second seminar on workers and adult education at MCTC; and in 1966 the International Organization of Consumers Unions held a four-day seminar on consumer education in developing countries in order to provide on-the-spot courses for women on specific topics such as weaving, sewing, and cooperative marketing.

EARLY YEARS OF DEVELOPMENT AID

What could Israel, as the host country of an international training center in the early 1960s, offer women from the less developed parts of the world? The answer probably lies primarily in Israel's twofold nature at the time as a developed and, concurrently, developing country. In contrast to other Western industrial countries, Israel faced certain conditions—such as a hot climate, a tendency toward soil erosion, and periods of drought— with which recently established countries also had to cope. Whereas the conditions in advanced countries were quite removed from the African students' own circumstances at home, Israel served as a living laboratory of community development: it was progressively advancing toward becoming a more developed country, thus allowing observers to draw comparisons and conclusions.[1]

Another explanation for Israel's appeal is its rather early involvement with development aid. Israel's formal international cooperation program was born in 1958, when a small department named MASHAV was established in the Foreign Ministry to oversee the provision of aid to developing countries. Before long, this department evolved into the largest division in the ministry, endowed with a significant budget. Between 1958 and 1969, slightly more than 13,000 foreign trainees came to Israel from African, Asian, Latin American, and Mediterranean countries. This was the highest ration of foreign trainees relative to national population in the world.[2] Because Israel lacked substantial financial resources in those years, it primarily offered technical assistance in agriculture and education instead. It provided aid both by sending field experts to developing countries and by organizing courses at various institutions in Israel.

And Sweden? In the early 1960s, Sweden's strong civil society helped produce and, later, sustain a (mostly) pro-aid public opinion. The Swedish government, on the other hand, was at that time often criticized—mainly by the labor movement—for lagging behind in terms of development aid. On November 14, 1960, for example, *Stockholms Tidningen* stated explicitly that Sweden's achievements were inadequate:

> [W]here does Sweden stand in Black Africa? All comparison with the Big Powers, yes even to big industrial countries such as West Germany and Japan, would be a mistake since we do not have the same means. But have we done nearly as much to penetrate Africa as for instance done by Israel or even Switzerland? Apparently not. Without exaggeration it can be said that Sweden from a diplomatic point of view is disastrously under-represented in all of the vast area of Black Africa. [...] There is also plenty of room for Swedish technical aid which in turn may create understanding for Sweden and Swedish social life. Even if the West would use more judgement in the future in the political battle between East and West, Sweden can gain good will and to some extent influence the development towards democracy. A condition for this would be that we have our own people on the spot to give information about Sweden.[3]

However, in spite of its slow start in setting up bilateral projects in Africa, during the 1960s Sweden saw a steep and continuous increase in this field. Within a decade Sweden and the other Nordic countries became the world's top donors, as measured on the basis of ODA/GNI (Official Development Assistance as a proportion of Gross National Income).[4] The underlying principles of Swedish development aid, stipulated in the Government 1962:100 Bill, included the promotion of economic growth, democracy, social equality, and independence. In many senses, this approach derived from a concept that may be termed "domestic analogy," namely the belief that the abovementioned fundamental values of Swedish society were indivisible, and that solidarity does not stop at national borders.[5] In its early years, Swedish development aid had two unique characteristics. First, Sweden granted a substantial portion of its development aid as multilateral aid, mainly through various UN institutions.[6] Second, the educational opportunities offered to students from developing countries in Sweden itself were limited to those fields in which Sweden could claim to have special expertise. For other fields, students were sent to countries better acquainted with the subject matter, preferably places with a similar climate and comparable conditions generally.[7]

SWEDISH-ISRAELI COOPERATION ON MCTC

The initial vision of combining Israeli and Swedish sources to provide development aid to Africa appeared explicitly in the two countries' labor movements. Operationally, however, Israeli-Swedish cooperation on MCTC is rooted in a joint initiative of three women: Golda Meir, Inga Thorsson, and Mina Ben-Zvi.

Golda Meir (1898–1978) was Israel's fourth prime minister, serving in that position from 1969 to 1974 (the only woman ever to become head of state in Israel). At a very young age, Meir became active in the Yishuv's (pre-state Israel's) labor movement, and later also in the Histadrut.[8] During her decade-long service as foreign minister (1956–1966), she became deeply involved in the establishment of MCTC, as she described in her autobiography, *My Life*:

> The Centre has always held a very special place in my heart, not only because I helped to found it, together with Sweden's Inga Thorsson and Israel's Mina Ben-Zvi, but also because I so greatly admire these women from developing countries who leave their towns and villages, and their families, and travel so far to a strange country in order to learn the skills that will eventually make the life of their people easier and richer. There is something heroic, I think – and this is not a word I use easily or often – in the effort made by such women to ensure a better and fuller existence for themselves, for their children and for their children's children through the long, difficult process of self-education.[9]

Initiating Israel's relations with the newly established African states was one of Meir's main contributions to Israeli foreign affairs. Meir was responsible for envisioning MCTC, appointing Mina Ben-Zvi as the center's director, providing guidance and consultations to the center—including in regard to its relationship with Sweden—and offering the center financial support whenever its original budget did not suffice.[10]

Inga Thorsson (1915–1994) was, in many senses, Golda Meir's counterpart on the Swedish side. Early in life Thorsson became active in the Swedish Social Democratic Party, and in 1952 she was appointed president of the Swedish Social Democratic Women's Federation as well as a member of Stockholm's City Council. Between 1964 and 1966 she served as Sweden's ambassador to Israel, thus becoming one of Sweden's first women ambassadors. In 1967 she became the director of the Social Development Division of the UN and was later appointed state secretary for disarmament issues and chairperson of the Swedish delegation to the UN Disarmament Conference in Geneva. Thorsson's career, very much like that of Golda Meir, had a solid trilateral basis: the labor movement, foreign affairs, UN.

Mina Ben-Zvi (1909–2000), the last key figure, immigrated to Palestine from Russia in 1921. In 1947 she was appointed head of the Histadrut's Immigrant Absorption Department in northern Israel. During the Second World War she served in the British Army in Egypt as company commander and three years later, during Israel's war of Independence, she established the Women's Corps of the Israel Defense Forces and became its first commanding officer. Interestingly, from 1953 to 1955, while accompanying her husband during his posting as Israeli Consul in Finland, she served in the organization Nativ, then an integral part of the Israeli Mossad, which was responsible for maintaining contacts with Jews behind the Iron Curtain and assisting their illegal immigration to Israel (Finland's proximity to the USSR was crucial).[11] At the same time, she strengthened her connections with international women's organizations, particularly with the UN Commission on the Status of Women, the Soroptimist International, and the International Council of Social Democratic Women. Ben-Zvi thus fused "her nationalist commitments with broader internationalist concern for advancing women's rights worldwide."[12]

All three women were active social democratic figures concerned with finding ways to provide suitable educational facilities for women in the recently established countries of Africa, a problem which first became internationally clear during the UN's seminar for African women held in Addis Ababa in 1960. Following this seminar, the three future founders of MCTC decided to invite women leaders from developing countries to a seminar on "The Role of Women in a Developing Society" that took place in Haifa, attended by 66 women from 23 countries, all holding positions of responsibility in their local communities or at national level. Upon returning from the seminar to Sweden, Inga Thorsson met with representatives from the Social Democratic Women's Federation, the Cooperative Movement, and the Trade Union Confederation (an umbrella organization for Swedish trade unions, commonly referred to as LO). Together, they adopted her recommendation to build a training center in Israel, rather than Sweden, since

> the knowledge in Sweden of problems and conditions in developing countries was too limited to make this kind of assistance useful. Our climate and culture and, above all, our advanced technical standards were also factors that were considered to make it difficult for women from developing countries to benefit from educational activities in Sweden.[13]

MCTC held its first board of directors meeting on June 4, 1963 in Jerusalem. Calling itself the Swedish-Haifa Committee, this body included three sets of parties: Inga Thorsson and Etti Widhe represented the three Swedish voluntary organizations, namely the Cooperative Movement, the Trade Union Confederation, and the Social Democratic Women's Federation; Mina Ben-Zvi and Moshe Fleeman represented the Haifa Municipality; and Aharon Remez and Moshe Carmiel represented MASHAV from the Israeli Foreign Ministry. The committee was not a legal instrument but rather a coordinating body, managed by all three parties.[14] The aim of the center, it was jointly decided, was to foster and promote educational and training facilities for women in fields of social importance to them as both citizens and workers in developing countries.[15] Throughout the years, the joint board met once a year (sometimes twice), and the meetings were of an informative as well as advisory character.[16]

Regarding the financing of MCTC, all parties were to contribute. In 1961, the Municipality of Haifa purchased a house for the center, located at 12 David Pinski street, Haifa (still in use today), for $150,000.[17] MASHAV undertook to participate mainly by way of maintenance and operating costs, and the Swedish organizations pledged to grant scholarships for African women. Additional scholarships were provided by specialized agencies of the UN, including UNESCO, UNICEF, WHO, and FAO, as well as other international organizations such as the Soroptimist movement.

Sweden's financial contribution to MCTC varied significantly over the years.[18] In all, the Swedish Social Democratic Women's Federation contributed a total of 340,660 SEK between 1963 and 1977; the Swedish Trade Union Confederation contributed a total of 233,458 SEK between 1963 and 1969; and the Cooperative Movement contributed a total of 715,704 SEK between 1963 and 1974. Cumulatively, the three voluntary organizations contributed 1,289,830 SEK ($248,522) over the course of fourteen years.[19]

However, the contribution from Swedish voluntary organizations was not enough for the needs of MCTC. Accordingly, in 1963 the Swedish government, through its Agency for International Development Cooperation (named NIB at the time and changed to SIDA in 1965), began to support MCTC with increasing contributions, while the contributions from the voluntary organizations decreased. This shift to government funding was initiated in 1962 by Inga Thorsson, who requested that NIB make Swedish scholarships available to women at MCTC. Soon thereafter, in 1963 and again in 1967, Sweden signed agreements with UNESCO to finance several activities aimed at increasing educational opportunities for women in Africa, including through scholarships to attend courses at MCTC.[20] In all, between 1963 and 1978, the Swedish government contributed a total of 9.2 million SEK ($1,772,639) to MCTC.[21]

Notably, the cooperation between Swedish organizations and MCTC entailed far more than the former's financial contribution: the Israeli-Swedish leadership of MCTC held frequent consultations, visits, and exchanges of views; MCTC's students were invited to take part in advanced study programs in Sweden; Swedish partners assisted MCTC in finding counterparts for the follow-up surveys on courses; MCTC's teaching staff included Swedish lecturers; MCTC hosted groups from Sweden's neighboring Nordic countries, including a group of fifteen Danish experts on development aid (1970) and a group of thirty-two Norwegian students from Oslo University (1971); Swedish organizations were responsible for publishing numerous articles on MCTC in national and international journals; and beginning in 1976, the Swedish-Haifa Committee took an active part in selecting course participants and disseminating information about the various courses of MCTC.

INTERNATIONAL COOPERATION

What drove Israel and Sweden to join forces, through MCTC, in providing development aid to Africa? From the viewpoint of the Israeli Foreign Ministry, strengthening relations with Sweden was an imperative aim. Severely lacking in international allies from the time of its establishment in 1948 (and even more so from 1955), Israel was continually seeking countries with whom it could ally. Given its constructive relations with Sweden (as well as the other Nordic countries) throughout the 1950s, Israel hoped to further reinforce these relations by working together on development aid projects.[22]

Another, and more implicit, aim for Israel in cooperating with Sweden might relate to what scholars term "signaling devices"—that is, senior Israeli officials wanted to convey to Sweden that Israel, though recently established, numbered among the developed, rather than developing, countries, and that Israeli society was advanced enough to be a partner worthy of cooperation.[23] Historian Daniel Kupfert Heller illustrated this signaling in his description of Mina Ben-Zvi's dual role as women's rights defender and "Israeli Ambassador" in international organizations:

> Ben-Zvi's activism also illuminates the ways in which Israeli officials utilized the discourse of women's advancement to help bring their country out of international isolation. When Israeli officials addressed the ICSDW [International Council of Social Democratic Women] and the UN's specialized agencies, they described their country's treatment of women as a window onto Israel's commitment to human rights and economic progress. This commitment, they argued, put them on par with countries in the West.[24]

Sweden had entirely different aims in relation to cooperation with Israel on MCTC. First, the joint project offered Sweden a way to become more involved in international affairs, thereby advancing a policy that had dominated Swedish politics since the end of the Second World War. While residual guilt over Swedish problematic neutrality during the war was clearly absent within Swedish political circles, a more active conduct toward international challenges and conflicts became prevalent. Second, Sweden wished to increase "grassroots" support for its emerging policy of providing aid to developing countries. In that respect, cooperation on MCTC "played an important role, when the Swedish development assistance programs first started, and it was vital to have the support for them from the Swedish public opinion."[25] Finally, and this was of utmost importance for Swedish officials, cooperation with Israel—a pioneer country in providing assistance to developing countries—enabled Swedish authorities, like SIDA, to profit from the experience of Israeli experts, who had already been working in this field for several years. Swedish representatives benefited from Israel's experience in Africa both indirectly, through the meetings of MCTC's joint board of directors, and directly, through MCTC courses designed specifically for Swedish development aid workers. In September–October 1966, for example, MCTC hosted a group of eleven Swedish volunteers, all professionally trained in early childhood education, a training officer from SIDA, and a representative from the Ministry of Community Development in Ethiopia (invited by SIDA).[26] Before arriving at MCTC, the volunteers completed a preparatory course in Sweden. They then came to Haifa for practical experience, after which they proceeded to Ethiopia in order to serve at health centers affiliated with the Swedish government's aid programs. One of the social highlights for this group was a celebration marking Lesotho's independence, held at MCTC and attended by high-ranking diplomats from the Swedish and Danish embassies as well as UN representatives.[27]

MCTC thus served as a training center not only for students from developing countries but also for trainers from developed countries, mainly Sweden and the other Nordic countries. Swedish experts with specializations in various areas of development aid regularly came to MCTC, sometimes in groups and sometimes as observers. In Haifa, they were able to receive both theoretical and practical guidance in aspects of development aid that the Swedish authorities were not able to offer them in their home country. In this sense, MCTC served as a bridge between Sweden and Africa.

Bilateral vs. Multilateral Aid

At the time of MCTC's inception, the Swedish voluntary organizations insisted that African women receive their scholarships through a special fund at UNESCO. The channeling of national grants in a multilateral manner, in this case through the UN, corresponded with prevalent views held by the Swedish public and government at the time. They believed that the use of UN organs to provide aid was an imperative means of proving not only Sweden's increasing engagement in international affairs but also its confidence in the leading role of international organizations in solving global challenges. Hence, in October 1963 the Swedish government made a contribution of $481,732 to UNESCO to finance six projects intended to extend educational opportunities for women in Africa. One of these projects was MCTC, for which 35–40 scholarships were awarded annually. UNESCO's representative, in response, expressed great appreciation for Sweden's generous contribution, describing it as "a fine example of international cooperation."[28]

Israel, however, focused mainly on bilateral, not multilateral, agreements with the various African countries to which it provided development aid. In so doing, it hoped not only to ensure the efficiency of its aid but also to strengthen these countries' sense of reciprocity with Israel, particularly through their UN voting pattern. Furthermore, many in Israel believed that the 13% treatment fee allocated to UNESCO for transferring the Swedish grants was a waste of money. Israeli efforts to change Swedish conduct were futile though: the Swedes insisted on having their multilateral assistance program operate through UNESCO. This state of affairs drew criticism in certain Israeli circles, including charges that while Sweden was "preaching" to the rest of the world (including Israel) on the utmost importance of providing aid through multilateral agreements with the UN, Sweden itself—except in the case of MCTC—was providing more than 51% of its development aid through bilateral agreements.[29]

Interestingly, over the years Sweden's approach underwent a drastic change. On May 5, 1966, during the fifth meeting of the Swedish-Haifa board of directors, the Swedish representative and chairperson, Anna Rudling, suggested—on behalf of SIDA's Director General Ernst Michanek—that the Swedish contribution be granted directly to MCTC rather than through UNESCO. Surprisingly, the center's director, Mina Ben-Zvi, was hesitant. In her opinion, UNESCO's involvement in the granting of scholarships created a positive impression among authorities in the receiving African countries. Foreign Minister Golda Meir, who also attended the meeting, further argued that the prestige of the scholarships would definitely be degraded if that no longer came through the UN. After a lengthy discussion, a solution was found: the scholarships project through UNESCO would continue as before, while the additional sum that SIDA was prepared to allocate to MCTC (for follow-up tours, on-the-spot courses, and special seminars) would be granted bilaterally.[30] And so it was.

While Sweden's request to terminate its contribution through UNESCO and grant it directly to MCTC probably stemmed from its wish to enhance its international profile as well as national presence in Africa, Israel, by then, had a strong reason to object. From the early 1960s, Arab states, led by Egyptian President Gamal Abdel Nasser, had been pressuring Arab states to condemn Israel in various international forums. Israel's first major disappointment in this regard occurred in January 1961, when Ghana's Prime Minister Kwame Nkrumah, who had been on very friendly terms with Israel, signed the Casablanca Declaration, a statement expressing a shared vision for Africa, which also contained condemnations of Israel. This set a pattern for African conduct on subsequent UN resolutions.[31] Most other African states, however, were reluctant to be drawn into what they regarded at the time as non-African affair and preferred to maintain ties with both Israel and the Arab states. Eventually, however, the Arab pressure bore fruit, resulting in the deterioration of Israel's political status in Africa: by the end of 1973 almost all African states had severed diplomatic ties with Israel. It was against this background that both Golda Meir as foreign minister and Mina Ben-Zvi as head of MCTC desperately needed the cloak of an international organization, such as the UN, for Israeli projects in Africa. The association of MCTC scholarships with a respectable and neutral organization such as UNESCO proved highly valuable in Israel's political considerations vis-à-vis Africa during the 1960s and early 1970s.

Social Democratic Development Aid

Early development aid provided by both Sweden and Israel was based on a social democratic outlook. For Sweden's part, the Swedish Social Democratic Women's Federation, the Trade Union Confederation, and the Cooperative Movement—the three Swedish voluntary organizations that initiated the collaboration with MCTC—were distinctly social democratic. They were all part of the Swedish labor movement and shared a similar worldview regarding the importance of women's participation in public life. Support for MCTC was only one of their enterprises in international development cooperation, which concentrated on the education of workers in general and that of trade union members in particular. This was also true for Sweden's formal policy at that time: it was offering courses to students from developing countries on topics such as community development, trade unionism, consumer education, and corporatism. According to historian Carl Marklund,

> [t]he corporatist arrangements of the post-war welfare state project greatly facilitated the forging of stable alliances between state-level ODA and civil society-level popular mobilization for Third World solidarity characteristic of Nordic humanitarian action during the Cold War.[32]

Israel also maintained a social democratic outlook. The interest among African states in modern techniques that Israel employed in various agricultural and industrial fields correlated with the social framework in which these techniques were practiced. Israel was a living laboratory of social democratic economic experiences in development and was willing to place its experience in cooperative endeavors at the disposal of people seeking to utilize it.[33] The cooperative and collective villages of Israeli workers—the *kibbutz* and the *Moshav*—became a special attraction.

It is evident that MCTC's curriculum was based on distinctly socialist premises, as the following three examples demonstrate. First, MCTC's popular course on adult education addressed the organization of literacy campaigns, methods for teaching adults, and the preparation of teaching materials. Its primary stated goal was to provide general education for adults, enabling them to become "useful and productive citizens" in accordance with the social democratic vision.[34] Second, many MCTC courses included study excursions to various socialist institutions, such as the Afro-Asian Institute for Cooperative and Labor Studies, located in Tel Aviv, the Cooperative Family Farm near Taanach, the Collective Settlement in Kibbutz Kfar Masaryk, and the Histadrut-affiliated Beit Berl—Adult Education College. For all these visits, the focus was on how organized labor and cooperative enterprises, especially in rural areas, could promote the profitability of social and economic development projects.[35] Third, a study tour on non-conventional approaches to education, conducted in October–November 1969, provided students with new methods and techniques for accelerating processes of learning "initiated under the pressure of national needs and development."[36] Throughout the study tour, special emphasis was placed on the *kibbutz* and the *moshav* as means of integrating new communities into a cooperative way of life. "Implicit throughout," so stated the course description, "was the motive not only to impart knowledge, professions and skills but also to guide the youth towards positive social values and attitudes."[37] Upon conclusion of the study tour, Sweden extended invitation to all participants to spend a week in Sweden and receive training in workers education, corporatism, and trade unionism. In a subsequent report, one participant summarized its relevance for her:

> Israel and Sweden [...] each has definitely a great deal to offer to developing countries in the provision of education related to the needs and circumstances of each. In both countries adult education has helped to shape the society [...] and has been organized by popular movements such as labour and cooperative movements.[38]

CIRCULATION OF KNOWLEDGE

Swedish-Israeli cooperation on MCTC facilitated the circulation of knowledge and experience regarding the early days of development aid, as provided by two main transferors: organizations and key figures. In terms of the former, various national and international organizations, all with a social democratic outlook as a common denominator, served as institutionalized sources of knowledge transfer. At the national level, these organizations included trade unions, local women's organizations, the Afro-Asian Institute for Cooperative and Labour Studies, SIDA, and the social democratic parties. Internationally, MCTC enjoyed the support of two prominent organizations: the International Labour Organization (ILO) and the International Council of Social Democratic women (ICSDW).

The ILO was established in 1919. Sweden joined it in 1920 and Israel in 1949. Through its cultivation and transmission of knowledge, the ILO had critical influence on the development of labor law and related social policies over the years.[39] Moreover, at the operational level, it launched programs to train workers from developing countries to become responsible as well as active citizens in the process of nation building. In 1946 it became the first United Nations specialized agency. The ILO's annual meetings provided a venue for Swedish and Israeli socialists to develop close relations. One of the outcomes of these contacts was the first Swedish training program for African women, launched in 1963 by the ILO in cooperation with FAO and UNESCO: MCTC was chosen as one of few training institutions to be sponsored by the ILO.[40]

Another important organization was the ICSDW, which is part of the Socialist International. The origins of the Socialist International trace back to the early international organizations of the labor movement in the mid-nineteenth century. After the rise of Nazism led to the dissolution of its predecessor in 1940, it re-emerged in 1951 as the Socialist International, a worldwide organization of social democratic, socialist, and labor parties, both in government and in opposition. In 1960, its supreme decision-making body, the Council, held its annual conference in Haifa, marking the first time that the Council met outside of Europe. More than 90 members from 21 countries were present, representing 60 million European voters at the time. The most salient topic during the Council's discussions was the substantial socialist engagement in providing aid to developing countries in Africa and in Asia. As Israel had by then earned a favorable international reputation as a solid source of know-how and problem-solving approaches in the provision of assistance to developing countries, its views received careful consideration.[41] By the end of the conference, it was decided that

> European Socialists will put all their knowledge in the organization of workers, in political education, in building a society, and all the knowledge of their peoples, technical and social knowledge, at the disposal of the great task – full freedom of man, political, economic and cultural, wherever he lives: freedom for all – regardless of race and religion.[42]

As noted, the second transferor of knowledge between Israel and Sweden on early aid provision was key figures, or more precisely: key women figures. Although a few men did play a role in MCTC's establishment and maintenance—for example Haifa's Mayor Abba Khoushy and the director (1960–1964) of the Israeli Association for International Cooperation, Aharon Remez—MCTC was undoubtedly a women's venture. Swedish and Israeli women conceived the vision of MCTC, founded it, and operated it throughout the years. Moreover, for many years, MCTC only invited and hosted women—from Africa, Asia, and Latin America—to take part in its courses.

Fascinatingly, the establishment of MCTC illustrates how these leading social democratic figures within different social democratic organizations interacted in order to pursue a shared aim based on a prominent principle of social democracy—internationalism: the quest for greater political and economic cooperation among states.[43] But how did this cooperation come about?

It all began in 1960, when Inga Thorsson embarked on a tour in Africa on behalf of Swedish Prime Minister Tage Erlander, in order to study local women's education opportunities. There, she met Israeli Foreign Minister Golda Meir during one of the latter's numerous visits to Africa as part of Israel's mission to strengthen relations with the newly established African states.[44] These two women had a very similar perspective on the ways and means of providing educational training for women in developing countries. By chance, Mina Ben-Zvi also met Inga Thorsson in 1960: while resting in a sanatorium in Zichron Yaakov, Israel, Ben-Zvi was approached by a woman sitting and reading next to her, and was asked for her opinion on the book *On the Beach*.[45] "In short, we somehow got into a conversation and became friends," said Mina Ben-Zvi twenty-eight years later.[46] This woman, Inga Thorsson, was visiting Israel at the time as the Women's Council representative to the Socialist International conference held, as mentioned, in Haifa in 1960.

Half a year later, and perhaps for reasons not entirely unrelated to this coincidental meeting, the International Council of Social Democratic Women appointed Mina Ben-Zvi as its representative to the UN's regional seminar for African women, to be held in Addis Ababa in December 1960. Before departing, however, Ben-Zvi was summoned to a meeting with Foreign Minister Golda Meir, who asked her to extend her visit in Africa so as to include Kenya, Tanganyika, and Uganda, with the aim of strengthening Israel's relations with them.[47] After Ben-Zvi's return from Africa, the plan for MCTC's establishment began to take shape. Inga Thorsson generated Swedish as well as UN interest and support in this planned venture, and soon thereafter, at the conclusion of a seminar on "The Role of Women in a Developing Society" convened in April 1961, in Haifa, all participants recommended that a permanent institute be set up in Haifa for the training of women in social services. Needless to say, Golda Meir's and Inga Thorsson's influence was instrumental in Mina Ben-Zvi's subsequent appointment as MCTC's director.

THE END OF SWEDISH-ISRAELI COOPERATION ON MCTC

In 1979, after sixteen years of support, SIDA decided unilaterally to terminate its cooperation on MCTC, at the time its longest cooperative development project.[48] This decision came as a great surprise, and no less of a disappointment, not only to MCTC staff but even in Sweden—to the Swedish women's voluntary organizations who were partners in the project. In an effort to reverse the decision, the latter decided to compile a detailed review of Sweden's cumulative contribution to MCTC over the years. In the review, which also covered general collaboration between Swedish non-governmental organizations and SIDA, they emphasized that

> [i]n retrospect it is easy to say that SIDA ought to have made sure its policy and, not least, changes in policy were well understood by the organizations. There is today a more continuous contact between women's organizations in Sweden and SIDA, than has ever been the case earlier. Hopefully this will help avoid something similar to happen again in the future.[49]

In response to this criticism and in an effort to ease the tensions that had emerged, SIDA suggested that its contribution be phased out over the course of a five-year period (until 1984) in order to guarantee a smooth transition and allow as little disruption as possible to MCTC already-scheduled activities. Having no other choice, the Swedish voluntary organizations had to comply.[50]

But what were the reasons behind SIDA's decision? What drove Sweden, after more than one and a half decades of close cooperation, to put a sudden end to it? Given that political relations between Israel and Sweden deteriorated during the 1970s, mainly as a consequence of the intensifying Israeli-Palestinian conflict, one might presume that the decision had a political background. It seems reasonable to deduce that following the war of 1967, and even more so after the war of 1973, Sweden's critique of Israeli conduct toward Palestinian refugees and land—and Israel's refusal to accept it—would lead to a significant reduction in Swedish-Israeli cooperation on MCTC. However, an in-depth analysis reveals four other reasons for SIDA's decision, none of them directly related to the changed political dynamics between the two countries.[51]

The first reason for Sweden's decision to terminate its cooperation on MCTC had to do with the gradual change in Sweden's development aid policy in regard to the training of women.[52] In a shift from the practice prevalent during the 1960s, in the 1970s Swedish training began to take place primarily in the trainees' home countries. Sweden started to invest in the establishment of training centers in Africa, and only when such an option was not feasible, did it offer training in another, preferably neighboring, country. When MCTC launched its educational program in 1961, the center was unique in the sense that no comparable training institutions existed elsewhere. As the years passed, however, institutions with a mandate similar to MCTC began to emerge in a number of developing countries, and with the loss of its uniqueness MCTC also lost its appeal to SIDA.

The second reason had to do with Israel's and Sweden's different geopolitical considerations. During the late 1960, and even more so following the war of 1973 and the intense Arab pressure, all African countries (except for Lesotho, Swaziland, and Malawi) severed their diplomatic ties with Israel. Consequently, it became increasingly difficult for MCTC to find African women who were willing to attend courses in Israel. Moreover, the United Nations Development Programme closed its Jerusalem office in 1976, posing another major difficulty for MCTC.[53] Until then, this UN office had been responsible for the dissemination of information on MCTC and the recruitment of candidates. After it closed, MCTC was unable to find a suitable substitute, as no other international organization had a comparable network or commanded the respect in Africa that the UN did. Facing these cumulative difficulties in maintaining its educational activities in the African continent, MCTC increasingly shifted its focus to students from developing countries in Asia and in Latin America with which Israel was then cultivating closer relations.

Sweden's relations with Africa, on the other hand, underwent a reverse trend. Since the early 1960s, Sweden had been continually increasing its development aid to Africa, in terms of both financial support and technical assistance. Slowly but surely, Sweden developed an international reputation as a leading provider of aid to Africa, while concurrently development cooperation in general became a matter of priority in Swedish international politics and an arena for particular activism and engagement.[54] Hence, while SIDA was looking for ways to strengthen its ties with African countries through development aid, Israel—having no other choice—needed to loosen them and turn to Latin America and Asia instead. In 1979, for example, only one of MCTC's numerous courses took place in a Swedish aid recipient country in Africa. SIDA viewed this fact as inconsistent with Sweden's foreign interests.[55]

The third reason was SIDA's reluctance to become the main funder of MCTC. According to SIDA's calculations, between 1961 and 1971 it was underwriting about 25% of MCTC's total expenses, but in the mid-1970s its contribution increased considerably, reaching approximately 40% in 1979. SIDA viewed it as unacceptable that it was providing such a large portion of the budget for a center in a developed (rather than developing) country. Another, albeit related, factor was that one of MCTC's principal stated goals was to present a positive picture of Israeli society, and SIDA refused to continue serving as a funder for Israeli foreign interests.[56]

Finally, everything is personal. The fourth reason was the generational shift. In 1979, MCTC's director, Mina Ben-Zvi, was 70 years old and nearing retirement. Golda Meir had passed away the year before, at the age of 80. Inga Thorsson and Anna Rudling were in their sixties. In MCTC's early years, the professional relations between these women—the founding leadership—quickly assumed a personal dimension as well, which became an integral aspect of increased Swedish-Israeli cooperation. An especially close relationship developed between Inga Thorsson and Mina Ben-Zvi, who, with their families, regularly spent their summer vacations at each other's. During a joint vacation in August 1963, for example, the two women traveled to Södermanland to visit Swedish Prime Minister Tage Erlander and his wife at their summer residence.[57] In later years, when both Golda Meir and Inga Thorsson held even higher-level political roles, the close relationship between Mina Ben-Zvi and Anna Rudling became the foundation and driving force of Swedish-Israeli cooperation on MCTC. They met not only at MCTC's annual joint board meetings but also, and frequently, at various international women's conferences. When SIDA decided to terminate its support to MCTC, it was Anna Rudling (together with two other women, Maj Karlberg, secretary of the Swedish-Haifa Committee, and Ulla Kann from the Institute of International Education at the University of Stockholm) who initiated and conducted the above mentioned in-depth study on Sweden's contribution to MCTC, in a futile attempt to reverse SIDA's decision. On the whole, Swedish-Israeli cooperation on MCTC was very much based on close personal relations. Once a generational shift occurred, the bilateral cooperation likewise diminished.

To conclude, Swedish-Israeli cooperation on MCTC was highly successful not only in terms of its influence on the lives of African women within their developing societies but also in strengthening bilateral Israeli-Swedish relations. The reason for this remarkable twofold success lies in the fact that both Israel and Sweden benefited greatly from this joint venture. The young Israeli state, lacking in financial resources and, no less, in international allies, benefited from Sweden's substantial budgetary supplement and the constructive interaction between the countries, and with the UN, that followed. For its part, Sweden, a relative latecomer to developed world's race to provide aid to recently established African states, benefited from Israel's pioneering experience in the field of development aid.

On a more general level, Swedish-Israeli cooperation on MCTC presents an intriguing case study of the circuitous ways in which knowledge spreads. Conveyed by key individuals, ideas and experience reached and circulated within diverse international organizations, and were then implemented in different ways in each national setting. Moreover, these organizations offered a valuable platform for building connections between local, national, and international authorities. Adopting this point of view, one might argue that the renowned "Swedish model" of development aid (later also referred to as the "Nordic model"), which was in its infancy in the early 1960s, developed under international—and, not least, specifically Israeli—influence.

Finally, the joint Swedish-Israeli venture of MCTC supports the claim that the labor movement of the 1960s and 1970s, working through its national and international organizations, was a forerunner in promoting Third World solidarity. It was not only the social democratic governments that played a decisive role, but also diverse socialist institutions that were instrumental in generating both official and public support for development aid. It is hardly surprising, therefore, that the close cooperation between Israeli and Sweden on MCTC was terminated in 1979, shortly after each country's long-standing social democratic government had to resign—in Sweden in 1976 and in Israel in 1977.

Acknowledgements I would like to thank David Stavrou for an impeccable translation of various documents from the SIDA archives, which was a great contribution to this study.

Notes

1. D. V. Serge, 'The Philosophy and Practice of Israel's International Cooperation', in *Michael Curtis and Susan Aurelia Gitelson*, eds. Israel in the Third World (New Brunswick and New Jersey: Transaction 1976), p. 12.
2. Ibid., p. 18.

3. Translated to English by the Israeli Embassy in Stockholm, 16 November 1960, ISA-mfa-Political–000k9os, Israel State Archives, Jerusalem.
4. Thorsten Borring Olesen, 'Scandinavian Development Policies', in *Peter Nedergaard and Anders Wivel*, eds. The Routledge Handbook of Scandinavian Politics (London and New York: Routledge, 2018), p. 294.
5. Ann-Marie Ekengren and Norbert Götz, 'The One Per Cent Country: Sweden's Internationalism of the Aid Norm', in *Thorsten Borring Olesen, Helge Ø. Pharo, and Kristian Paaskesen*, eds. Saints and Sinners—Official Development Aid and Its Dynamics in a Historical and Comparative Perspective (Oslo: Akademisa Publishing Norway, 2013), pp. 34–35. Olesen, 'Scandinavian Development Policies', p. 294.
6. Ibid.
7. Ekengren and Götz, 'The One Per Cent Country', pp. 24–25.
8. For a detailed description of Golda Meir's early years in the labor movement, see Pnina Lahav, '"A Great Episode in the History of Womanhood": Golda Meir, the Women Workers' Council, Pioneer Women, and the Struggle for Gender Equality', *Israel Studies*, 23, no. 1 (2018), pp. 1–25.
9. Golda Meir, *My Life* (New York: G. P. Putnam's Sons, 1975), p. 333.
10. See interview with Mina Ben-Zvi, 7 June 1988: http://www.goldameir.org.il/index.php?dir=site&page=archives&op=item&cs=145 (accessed 3 January 2024).
11. Mina Ben-Zvi's retirement form, A581/126, Central Zionist Archives, Jerusalem.
12. Daniel Kupfert Heller, 'Israeli Aid and the "African Woman": The Gendered Politics of International Development, 1958–73', *Jewish Social Studies*, 25, no. 2 (2020), p. 53.
13. A Review of the Collaboration between Swedish Non-Governmental Organisations and the Swedish International Development Authority, SIDA, Sida Biståndskontoret Sri Lanka, SE/RA/420714, serie F36, vol. 10, pp. 7–8.
14. Minutes of the first meeting of the board of directors of the Carmel International Women's Centre, 4 June 1963, Jerusalem, MCTC Archives, Haifa.

15. ISA-mfa-InterCooperation-000796n, p. 190, Israel State Archives, Jerusalem.
16. A Review of the Collaboration between Swedish Non-Governmental Organisations and the Swedish International Development Authority, SIDA, p. 38.
17. Mary Saran, *For Community Service: The Mount Carmel Experiment* (Oxford: Basil Blackwell, 1974), p. 9.
18. The following two paragraphs are based on the information provided in 'A Review of the Collaboration between Swedish Non-Governmental Organisations and the Swedish International Development Authority, SIDA', pp. 9–10.
19. In 1963, one USD was worth 5.1935 SEK. Source: https://fxtop.com/en/historical-currency-converter.php?A=1&C1=SEK&C2=USD&DD=01&MM=04&YYYY=1963&B=1&P=&I=1&btnOK=Go%21.
20. A Review of the Collaboration between Swedish Non-Governmental Organisations and the Swedish International Development Authority, SIDA, p. 25.
21. PM (Promemoria) Nr. 48, 25 July 1979, vol. F1 ACA: 1131, p. 3, Sida Central Archives, Stockholm.
22. See the chapter on 'Ben Gurion, the Nordic Countries and the Neutral Bloc' in this book.
23. See, for example, Assaf Likhovski, 'Argonauts of the Eastern Mediterranean: Legal Transplants and Signaling', *Theoretical Inquiries in Law* 10, no. 2 (2009), pp. 619–51.
24. Kupfert Heller, 'Israeli Aid and the "African Woman"', p. 71.
25. A Review of the Collaboration between Swedish Non-Governmental Organisations and the Swedish International Development Authority, SIDA, p. 10.
26. Fanette Modek, 'Course for Swedish Volunteers, 8th September–8th October, Summary', 14 October 1966, MCTC Archives, Haifa.
27. Ibid.
28. 'Sweden Offers Nearly $500,000 to UNESCO to Help Educate African Women', press release no. 2424, 23 October 1963, Paris, ISA-mfa-InterCooperation-000796n, p. 95, Israeli State Archives, Jerusalem.
29. Dov Shmorak, First Secretary at the Israeli Embassy in Stockholm, to MASHAV, cited in a letter to Mina Ben-Zvi, 5 November 1964,

MCTC Archives, Haifa. It is indeed noteworthy, that by the 1970s Sweden had a far lower proportion of multilateral programs, as a percentage of all of its assistance programs (ca. 35 per cent), than did Norway, Denmark, and Finland (ca. 45 per cent). See Nils Andren, 'The Nordic Countries and North–South Relations', in Erik Allradt, Nils Andren, Sten Sparre Nilson et al. eds. *Nordic Democracy* (Copenhagen: Det Danske Selskab, 1981).
30. Minutes of the fifth meeting of the joint board of directors of the Mount Carmel International Training Centre, 5 May 1966, Folkets Hus, Stockholm, MCTC Archives, Haifa.
31. Gitelson, 'Israel's African Setback', p. 184.
32. Carl Marklund, 'Neutrality and Solidarity in Nordic Humanitarian Action' (Humanitarian Policy Group Working Paper, Overseas Development Institute, UK, January 2016), pp. 15–16.
33. Mordechai E. Kreinin, 'Israel and Africa: The Early Years', in *Curtis and Gitelson*, eds. Israel in the Third World, p. 58.
34. Mount Carmel International Training Centre for Community Services (Haifa, May 1966), p. 18.
35. See Akiva Eger, Director of the Afro-Asian Institute for Cooperative and Labour Studies, 'Crucial Problems of Development in the Third World', lecture, reprinted in Study Tour on Programmes for the Education of Adults, February–March 1971 (Haifa: Mount Carmel Training Centre for Community Services, 1971), pp. 79–83.
36. Foreword, in Study Tour on Non-Conventional Approaches to Education, 12 October to 22 November, 1969 (Haifa: Mount Carmel Training Centre for Community Services, 1969), p. 1.
37. Ibid.
38. Ibid., p. 123.
39. Pauli Kettunen, 'The Nordic Model and the ILO', in Norbert Götz and Heidi Haggren (eds), *Regional Cooperation and International Organizations: The Nordic Model in Transnational Alignment* (London and New York: Routledge, 2009), p. 76.
40. Saran, For Community Service, p. 92.
41. 'Representatives of Sixty Million', Davar, 29 April 1960, p. 35 [Hebrew].
42. Meir Bareli, 'The Role Is Still Big', Davar, 6 May 1960, p. 24 [Hebrew].

43. For a recent examination of this under-researched topic, see Alan Granadino, Stefan Nygård, and Peter Stadius, eds. *Rethinking European Social Democracy and Socialism: The History of the Central-Left in Northern and Southern Europe in the Late 20th Century* (London: Routledge, 2022).
44. Saran, For Community Service, p. 6.
45. This 1957 post-apocalyptic book (by British author Nevil Shute) looks at the lives of people awaiting the arrival of deadly radiation that was released during a nuclear war a year earlier. Each character in the novel deals with the impending death differently. Though clearly fictional, this book correlates with Thorsson's other life-long political battle, namely, opposition to Sweden acquiring nuclear weapons.
46. See interview with Mina Ben-Zvi, 7 June 1988, p. 3: http://www.goldameir.org.il/index.php?dir=site&page=-content&cs=245&lan gpage=heb (accessed 25 January 2022).
47. Ibid., p. 2.
48. A Review of the Collaboration between Swedish Non-Governmental Organisations and the Swedish International Development Authority, SIDA, p. 29.
49. Ibid., p. 47.
50. Ibid., p. 43.
51. It is noteworthy that from the 1980s onwards, MCTC underwent a major shift both in the identity of its recipient countries and in the nature of its offered aid, which helped it to adapt to the changing inner-political climate in Israel.
52. Ibid., p. 28.
53. Ibid., p. 26.
54. Sunniva Engh, 'The "Nordic Model" in *International Development Aid*', in Haldor Byrkjeflot, Lars Mjøset, Mads Mordhorst, and Klaus Petersen eds. The Making and Circulation of Nordic Models, Ideas and Images (London: Routledge, 2021), p. 125.
55. PM (Promemoria) Nr. 48, 25 July 1979, vol. F1 ACA: 1131, pp. 9–11, Sida Central Archives, Stockholm.
56. A Review of the Collaboration between Swedish Non-Governmental Organisations and the Swedish International Development Authority, SIDA, p. 26; see also PM (Promemoria)

Nr. 48, 25 July 1979, vol. F1 ACA: 1131, p. 10, Sida Central Archives, Stockholm.
57. Diary of Mina Ben-Zvi, A581/4, Central Zionist Archives, Jerusalem.

CHAPTER 7

Mission: The North. Concluding Travel Notes from Scandinavia

Abstract The conclusion chapter will be presented through texts written by four Israelis who for various reasons have visited the Scandinavian countries during the 1950s: Prime Minister David Ben Gurion, Nobel Prize winner in literature Shmuel Yosef Agnon, Historian (and wife of the Israeli Ambassador to Stockholm) Leni Yahil, and the young journalist Alex Carmel. Their varied perspectives, sometimes unexpectedly funny, illustrate the contemporary fascinating image that Israelis had on the Nordic countries. These texts also reflect the diversity of topics covered throughout the book.

Keywords Leni Yahil · David Ben Gurion · Shmuel Yosef Agnon · Alex Carmel · Nordic countries · Lapland

This concluding chapter offers a different viewpoint on the beginning of relations between the Nordic countries and Israel; not that of politics, alliances, movements, and ideology, but rather that of the individual, the common man. It presents the travel notes of four different Israelis who visited the northern countries during the 1950s and 1960s: Leni Yahil, David Ben Gurion, Shmuel Yosef Agnon, and Alex Carmel. Their perspectives are particularly diverse: first, that of a woman, a Holocaust researcher who lived in Sweden for three years as the wife of the Israeli ambassador,

© The Author(s), under exclusive license to Springer Nature Switzerland AG 2024
O. Keren-Carmel, *Nordic Traces in Israel*,
https://doi.org/10.1007/978-3-031-75287-2_7

and therefore her impressions are mainly political and thus more nuanced; followed by that of a prime minister on an official visit full of experiences; then the point of view of one of Israel's greatest writers who focuses—in his life as well as in his writing—on Judaism and its various communities abroad, and finally that of a young student with an extraordinary sense of humor during an eventful trip to Europe.

The stories of the four writers usually begin with similar themes: the breathtaking northern landscape, the different culture and habits of the Scandinavians compared to that of the Israelis, and not least—the cold weather. Then, however, each writer refers to topics related to his personal interests, which left strong impressions on him/her. Yahil focuses on the Scandinavian labor movement, Ben Gurion emphasizes the emerging political relations between Israel and the northern countries, Agnon seeks the image of the non-Israeli Jew, and Alex Carmel highlights the exotic aspects of unique Swedish customs. Although they visited the same countries during the same decade, the travel descriptions of the four writers thus stand out precisely because of their differences. Enjoy your reading.

Leni Yahil

Leni Yahil (1912–2007) was an internationally renowned Holocaust researcher. She wrote her doctoral thesis on the rescue of Danish Jews in the Holocaust and later published a comprehensive study that gained great resonance, titled "The Holocaust: The Fate of the Jews of Europe 1932–1945." But before her academic career, between 1956 and 1959, Yahil lived in Sweden, together with her husband Chaim Yahil—who was a senior diplomat in the Jewish Agency and later in the Israeli Ministry of Foreign Affairs, and served in those three years as Israel's envoy to Sweden, Norway, and Iceland (during his tenure the relationship between Israel and Sweden was upgraded and he became an ambassador)—and their two children, Amos and Jonathan. Back in Israel, she published her impressions under the title "Light and Shadow in the Northern Countries" in the monthly *Dvar Hapoelet*.[1] This monthly began its activity in the 1930s, first as a supplement to the newspaper *Davar*, and in 1950 as an independent newspaper, with the aim of integrating the women's rights movement into the emerging national society in Israel. Yahil's impressions indicate a deep familiarity with Swedish society in those years, and differ in essence from the typical impression of tourists who visited the country for a short period of time.

Wonders of landscape and climate, noble human figures, a society that seeks freedom and social justice, an exemplary democratic regime - this is how those countries are depicted in our minds. And above all, we remember the miracle, of which news had reached us like a ray of light in the darkness of the Second World War - the rescue of the Danish Jews, who were in danger of deportation by the Nazis, and the opening of Sweden's borders to them. However, those who get to know these wonderlands closely come to know that the reality is indeed much different from all those imaginary hallmarks, and yet there is some truth in them.

...First of all, it should be known that the Scandinavian countries and their inhabitants - although they indeed belong to the same family - are not at all made of the same skin. The appearance is different and the character is different. Here is little Denmark, which still belongs to the continent of Europe, takes part in its historical and cultural development, and maintains strong ties with all its northern neighbors. The landscape is soft and its people are both pleasant and full of humor, they are world-renowned farmers and sophisticated merchants, hospitable and they seldom talk, they like the hint (and if you didn't understand it - it's your fault), their soul is isolated from within, their great philosopher is Kierkegaard, whose loneliness seems to be the source of his quarry. Nevertheless, Denmark's cooperative organization is one of the best in the world.

Its big sister across the strait, S w e d e n, is different: a country of vast dimensions, rich in natural resources, and the landscape - except for the south, which is similar to Denmark - serious, heavy, infinite forest areas, plains strewn with rocks, tens of thousands of lakes. In the Middle Ages, there were times when great Sweden was subject to little Denmark, but in the 16th century it managed to break free. For the most part, its face was turned eastward, to the Baltic Sea, and its main frictions were with its big neighbor Russia, which threatened her to this day. The Swedes are the most restrained people among the Scandinavians, the coldest, who have rational considerations, the most cautious and also the most prone to drunkenness. Its sister-countries treat it with respect as well as suspect.

Everything that has ever been told about the wondrous landscape of the north pales to the sight of the mountains of N o r w a y and its fjords. There is a possibility that the mountains made an effort together to show you their vastness and infinity. In this country, which is indeed narrow but very long (the distance from the capital Oslo to the northern tip of Norway is the same distance like from Oslo to Naples), lives a small people numbering three and a half million. This is a brave people of seafarers, who turned their constant struggle with cruel nature - the latter seems constantly to overcome it - into an unfailing source of activity and invention, of spiritual inspiration and physical health.

...Sweden is the most interesting in terms of its social and economic organization. The Swedes are the masters of organization, and thanks to this they are placed at the head of the industrial nations - although their number is only seven and a half million, they are also among the most advanced in organizing their country as a "welfare state" (or as usually referred to as "charity state"). Social insurance dominates all areas of life: work, health, education, and care for old age. It is too difficult to detail all its ways and methods, but we will try to make several comments about the effect of this material and social insurance on the life of the family and society. The fighting instinct seems to have been taken away from the individual and the general public. To this normal internal state must be added the fact that for over 150 years it has not been forced to stand for itself in a war against an external enemy. Where is the human energy directed then? What are the fears, aspirations and hopes of the human beings here?
There are two tendencies among the Swedish people, and they have not yet reached unity and perfection: on the one hand - the tradition of the people and the patterns created in the past, and on the other hand - the renewal of society and its organization through up-to-date science and technology. In the last 50 years, production methods and lifestyles have changed from end to end. This revolution - which passed over the country without the use of any force other than the will of man, his intelligence and his work - left the Swede amazed but also wondering about his actions. The results do not correspond to the concepts according to which the people led their lives for hundreds of years, and the way to translate those concepts to the new reality of life has not yet been found.
Family life, for example, was conducted in Sweden in patriarchal patterns, perhaps longer than in the rest of Europe. But modern life destroyed them. About a quarter of all married women also work outside home, although in this industrialized country - which actually has a constant shortage of working hands - it is almost impossible to get a maid - and that's why their children are known as "key children" - who have the house key tied around their neck so they can enter the house when no one is there to welcome them. This situation is common in all strata of society, and especially among the workers. The number of women who work because they have an interest in the profession is not small, of course, but the number of those who want to improve their homes with modern machinery, buy a nicer apartment, go on trips to foreign countries, etc. is much greater. This tendency is not unique to Sweden, but there it is more pronounced. The materialistic ambitions are constantly increasing, and the fact that the home is being emptied of its content is probably also one of the reasons for the recent juvenile crime, which has spread in Sweden like an epidemic, and accompanied by very alarming phenomena in the area of sex life. This

chapter is very long and complicated, and things got to the point where the Ministry of Social Affairs (whose duties are broader than the duties of our Social Ministry) saw the need to contact women's organizations in order to get advice on how to handle the problem. But it is not only within the family that the relationship between man and his environment is lacking. There were very fixed traditional patterns for social relations in Sweden, and since these no longer fit the modern way of life - a crisis arose. Only one of the modern technical inventions came to serve society's relations - the telephone. Every Swede, as well as every Scandinavian, likes to call, because here the phone is not a useful device for short conversations, but a substitute for social life and direct contact between one person and another.

It goes without saying that a lot of energy is poured into constructive channels of various kinds. There are women's associations dedicated to numerous roles inside and outside the country. The energy invested in everything that might make practical life easier and give it a nicer shape is also very great. There really is a cult of the beautiful form. It is no coincidence that the Scandinavian countries are leading the way in all areas of interior architecture. In everything that is used in the house, the degree of attention paid to every detail, every corner, every arrangement, so that it will be more comfortable and more beautiful - is difficult to describe. But with all the positivity that exists in all that ornament, all that comfort, all that social security, one should not ignore a certain emptiness. There are no great roles and tasks that will unite the people in a common aspiration. More than once the Israeli who finds himself here can hear a strange statement: "We envy you."

DAVID BEN GURION

David Ben Gurion (1886–1973), Israel's first prime minister and leader of Mapai (Israeli Social Democratic Party), did not often leave the country during his many years in office. Nevertheless, during August 1962, he left, together with his wife Pola and their daughter Renana, for a four-week reciprocal visit to the five Nordic countries, following the visit of the prime ministers of Denmark, Norway, and Sweden to Israel between November 1961 and March 1962. *Kol Ha'am* newspaper, mouthpiece of the Communist Party in Israel, reported on the visit in a critical tone:

> [The prime minister] said that the visit to the 5 countries is not a state visit, but only an official visit, and that he does not want to achieve anything in this visit, except for mutual understanding. But it was precisely Ben

Gurion's official and unofficial companions who announced the pretentious goals that the Prime Minister set for himself during his trip to Scandinavia. "Davar" [the newspaper of Mapai - the governing party - O.K.C] of the 21st of this month reveals that one of Ben Gurion's goals is to bring together the heads of the social democratic governments and establish a kind of political bloc of the small countries. This is a goal that is not at all modest, but a goal that proves the initiator's arrogant grandiosity, which does not match either the power or the interest of Israel.[2]

Despite the negative tone, this interpretation was not completely inaccurate. However, Ben Gurion's high expectations from the visit were not realized: the Scandinavian prime ministers did not agree to add Israel to the Nordic bloc. When he returned to Israel, Ben Gurion convened a special meeting of the government,[3] which he devoted mainly to sharing his impressions from the northern countries. Reading it carefully, it is possible to recognize in Ben Gurion's coverage the remnants of his disappointment at the unsatisfactory results of the visit.

> Visiting five countries at once - it's a bit too much, although to a large extent there are repetitions - the same ceremonies, the same speeches, the same talking, but still it's too much.
> ... Then there are Jews in these places, that was the only torture I had. I talk to the Jews about Israel, all my companions also talk about this topic, and then we need to talk again, I have to think every time how not to repeat things that others have already said, I guess I succeeded in this matter.
> ... In one place there was a strange thing, it was in Finland, also there is an association for friendship with Israel, I thought they would surely speak Finnish - this is a language that no one in the world knows, and they did, but I was surprised by a woman that translated the words into Hebrew, I saw that she was holding a note written in Latin letters from which she was reading the translation of the speech, I thought that someone had written this translation for her in Latin letters. When she finished, I asked her if she understood Hebrew and she answered me in fluent Hebrew. A woman about 60 years old, I said to her: I hear you know Hebrew, how did you learn it, and she answered: I am interested in Judaism and I studied Hebrew. It turned out that she is a non-Jew married to a Jew, her Jewish husband does not know a word of Hebrew. He has a son who is a high official at the Foreign Ministry, where he hides his Jewishness. In Finland there was a big turmoil, when I came to the Foreign Ministry, and he did not hide his Jewishness from me, he talked to me as Jew.

...I also explained to them the matter of providing aid to the new countries. In one matter, they have a unique approach, the same position is indeed held by America, but with America it is only a pretense, America is advocating as if everything should be done through the United Nations, but when there is a matter concerning her own affairs - not infrequently she forgets about the existence of the United Nations. But they take the existence of the United Nations seriously. It is a difficult matter for them, it is a matter concerning the whole world. Helping new peoples is a general concern. It has to be done by the United Nations. I explained to them why we are not doing this through the United Nations, why at the moment we are more successful than others. I did not tell them that they should cooperate with us, but I explained to them why this should be done. They told me that the Labor movement would probably cooperate with us, but they, as countries, they cannot do this. It is like an attack on the United Nations. This is the business of the United Nations, they give money to the United Nations for this action. This will also be discussed in the Nordic Council. They said they would propose that it will be done by the Labor movement.
...The countries are similar to each other and different from each other. There is a lot of similarity between them all, socialist governments in all these countries. In some matters they are better than us, it is not the result of the situation that they are more advanced, but that they are richer. Even Norway, which is considered a poor country, is richer than us. Regarding Sweden, there is nothing to say. The social level that prevails there is utopian for us. Every person is secured from birth to death, at the age of 67 he retires, although he can continue to work. We in Israel also have to look into the issue of retirement.
...Individualism is very common, first of all - there are no villages because there is no need, there is complete security. Each farmer has his own piece of land, in the center of his land stands his house, he lives alone, for the most part self-employed, it is also difficult to get hired laborers, the agriculture is very extensive, primitive, mainly pasture, some wheat, not in all places, therefore they do not need laborers, but the units, the individualism is a revelation in itself.
...Iceland - a desert, worse than our desert [the Negev - O.K.C], it's all covered with lava, rocks, there are few areas where there is soil and you can sow and plant, these parts are cultivated. [...] In Iceland it is very cold, but they have a blessing, what nature has done, how God - blessed be He - arranges things: they have endless boiling water, trains are pulled by the boiling water, from that they have electricity. It is also a brave people, patriots, do not want other people to settle among them. I was told that in 930 they established the first parliament, there were seventy people, those

were the inhabitants of the entire island. They all gathered in one place and it was the first parliament, like the first conference of Poalei Zion in the Land of Israel [The Workers of the Land of Israel - O.K.C], we were about 120 people, all came on foot. A parliament in their language is called ALTHING, that means an assembly of everyone, this was their parliament, they gathered and decided, they boast that it is the first parliament in the world.

...I didn't really understand what is the source of the friendship [of the northern countries towards Israel - O.K.C.]. In some countries - the Bible. The Bible is more common there than among other European nations. I am not saying more than in England, but not only that. Not only their heads of states, but the whole peoples, the King of Sweden is especially interested, but not only him, not only the prime ministers, but the whole people. The newspapers were full of news about Israel and the visit. They had a visit by Nehru, the newspapers did not devote as much space to him as to our retinue. I saw love, friendship among all the people, among the youth and among the women. When we arrived at a certain place, a large crowd was waiting for us. It's hard to explain.

...One more thing. Despite the friendship - really deep, true and sincere friendship, there is admiration for the strength of Israel's endurance. A small nation surrounded by enemies, the talent of working in the desert, here we do things they don't. I admired their things and they admired ours. But friendship is not the same as identification, in this we need to educate our public. A people does not identify with another people, it does not want everything we want. Don't be tempted to think that a friend does everything we want. They have their own affairs. Things that concern them, their internal relationships. For example, they know that Sweden is neutral, none of these countries will do anything that would harm Sweden's neutrality. The Finns hate the Russians to death, but there are friendly political relations between them, and the other nations know that, they will not do anything to accentuate the Finns' hatred of the Russians, they will not do anything to put Finland in an uncomfortable position with Russia. It is possible that these considerations will bring them to an opposite position than we want, they will take a position according to their own considerations or according to international considerations, as they understand them.

...It is indescribable what they built in Sweden, they are neutral, there was no war on their land for 150 years, more than in Switzerland, what they spend on security - it's unbelievable, they built a city under the rock, under 120 meters of granite, a complete city with all the arrangements that people could live there for a year, there is water, air conditioning, hot water and cold water, all the comforts. At the moment it is used as a parking place for cars, they have a lot of cars and have no place to park them. Not all the people of Stockholm will be able to enter this underground city, only 17,000 people, but they will have all the normal needs, clinics, books, everything necessary. All this costs tens of millions of dollars and that's a neutral people. They build their own high-end jet planes, create all the other weapons and spend hundreds of millions of dollars. I asked them: You are a neutral people, why do you need all this? And the answer was: we need to be able to protect ourselves.

SHMUEL YOSEF AGNON

Shmuel Yosef Agnon (1887–1970) was one of the greatest modern Hebrew writers, and the only Israeli to win the Nobel Prize for Literature so far (1966). His many writings deal with the Jewish people, Israel and the Diaspora, and they have been greatly appreciated around the world.

On June 18, 1951, Agnon and his wife Esther, both over sixty years old, took off to Stockholm. It was the first time in their lives that they flew in a plane. The purpose of the visit in the Swedish capital was to promote the interests of Agnon by spreading his publications internationally, while hoping that this may advance his chances of winning the Nobel Prize for Literature (which he indeed won, but only 15 years later). In a letter to their son, Hemdat, he detailed his deep impression of the city: the bridges, the clean streets, the abundance of flowers, the beautiful houses made of bricks of various colors, the good manners of the residents, the silence that prevail everywhere, and the youthful appearance of the adults: "You see a man departing his home, walking like a 25 years old, and you wonder that his head is full with white hair, meaning that old people aged 55 are similar in their walking to young men."[4]

During the stay, on July 5, a reception in honor of Agnon was held at the home of Israel's envoy to Sweden, Avraham Nissan, with the participation of Swedish writers, journalists and various public figures. Below is the speech that Agnon gave during the ceremony, which describes in his unique way his impressions of the visit so far, while emphasizing—as a Jew born outside the Land of Israel—the Jews of the Diaspora and their unique culture.[5]

> For many years, I longed to see the northern countries. Legends that I read in my youth, stories and plays that I read as a young man drew me to these lands, to the mountains and hills and ravines and forests and bays

and rivers and lakes, which these lands are full of. And above the charms of creation, my heart was drawn to the inhabitants of these countries, which the poets spoke of. And here in the home of the Israeli envoy I thank you for all the pleasure and enjoyment I had from Scandinavian poetry.

One more thing brought me closer to the inhabitants of these countries, praises I heard from people who visited here. Anyone who visited the Scandinavian countries often speaks in praise of their inhabitants, that they are pleasant and their actions are pleasant. I don't know if they exaggerated, and if they did, then the exaggeration itself is important. And the inhabitants of these countries are like their kings and ministers. According to our Jewish tradition, every nation behaves as its king and ministers behave with Israel. If they behave towards Israel with respect and honesty, it means that they themselves are honest and honorable, and who else, like the kings of Scandinavia and their ministers, behave so well with us. And last year, when Dr. Wilhelm the chief rabbi invited me to come to Sweden, I said I will go and see these countries and their charms and I will also see our brothers, the children of Israel, who have found haven in them.

Lest you say that there is a lack of Jews in the Land of Israel that you bothered to come here? But I tell you, every person from Israel was created against a letter in the Torah, so knowing more Jews adds to knowing more letters in the Torah. And if I were not afraid of saying something that our predecessors did not say, I would claim, that Israel in the Land of Israel is the letters in the Torah, and Israel outside the land of Israel is the punctuation that shakes the letters. And like the scripture says, we will make thee borders of gold with studs of silver.

And when I decided to go to Scandinavia, I went to say farewell to my favorite places in Jerusalem and to my close relatives and friends. As I was about to say goodbye, I began to wonder how it is possible to leave such places and such people? And since I started to wonder, I started to hesitate if it was worth going away. And I was already close to canceling my trip and I saw in the act of canceling a kind of heroism, that after all the hesitations I had, I finally give up on the trip.

But it was already written in the travel book above that this so-and-so already started the journey. At the time I decided to cancel my trip, I entered the prayer house of the followers of Breslau and found them sitting as one, and at their head someone reading to them the stories of the late Rabbi Nachman about a king's daughter who was in captivity. Several heroes came and every one of them said, I can free the king's daughter of captivity. One brave man, with his hands cut off, said, I will free the king's daughter of captivity. They said to him, what is your special power? He said to them, I can shoot an arrow to great distances. They told him, this is not heroism. He repeated and said, the arrow that I shoot can return

to the bow. They told him, this is not heroism. As the reader reads and I hear, I said in my heart, I wonder if the words were not meant for me. If returning an arrow to the bow is not heroism, what is heroism in cancelling a trip? Rather, I will go and travel and see some of our brothers in the diaspora. And when I made up my mind to travel, I saw my journey as a kind of commandment. [...]
I cannot speak to you either in the holy language or in the Swedish language, the holy language because you are not used to it, the Swedish language because I do not know it. And if I want to talk to you, I need to talk to you in the language of a nation that has made itself blind to Israel's troubles [Agnon means the German language - O.K.C]. Therefore, my words will only include greetings.
Well, welcome and be blessed for coming. I know that you did not come in honor of me, but in honor of Jerusalem, where I come from. I pray that the right of Jerusalem will stand for me and for you and that we will see the benefit of Jerusalem in God's return, the return of Zion soon in our days, Amen.

Later on in his visit, Agnon accepted the invitation of Avraham Brody, an orientalist and philologist, to visit Norway with him (at that time Agnon's wife Esther went to visit her sister in London). On July 17, Brody and Agnon set out on their way to Norway, and it seems that Agnon was finally able to shed his worries: "Far from his wife, cut off from almost any familiar environment, amidst breathtaking landscapes, Agnon was able to completely free himself from the constraints of family, society, writing and publishing—and indulge himself fully to the charm and beauty and mystery that surrounded him from all sides."[6] During the visit to Lillehammer, Agnon wrote to his childhood friend Gershom Scholem in Jerusalem a poem [in Hebrew it rhymes] about his experiences from the visit, in a quite uncharacteristic style:

> God in the sky will send his greetings/ to the man of peace [Shalom - O.K.C] who sits in his place/ and does his daily work/ and I enjoy nights like days/ among rivers of water and maritime gulfs/ and travel and go and descend like an arrow/ between mountains and hills and wooden huts/ and celebrate not like you all kinds of orgies/ with Swedish, Danish and Norwegian women/ I do not know unfortunately if they are virgins/ but their hair is blond and their eyes are blue/ may my good deeds not be diminished on the Day of Judgment/ for the blue eyes and the blond hair/ pray for me [...]/ Sha"i Agnon .[7]

The end of Agnon's visit to Scandinavia was gloomy. At the end of August, after his return from Norway, Agnon suffered a heart attack and was hospitalized in Stockholm. After five weeks, the Agnon couple went to a small town called Hultafors in southwestern Sweden, in order to rehabilitate and rest. Agnon suffered there from loneliness—there were only gentiles around him and not a single Jew. And not only that, a few days before their return to Israel, in November, Agnon was informed that the decision of the Swedish Academy regarding the Nobel Prize had been made, and that this year the Swedish writer Pär Lagerkvist would receive it. This is how his wife Esther summed up the journey: "We learned that it is better for us to stay at home."[8]

ALEX CARMEL - A. TREMPAI

In December 1958 a new column began to be weekly published in *Maariv*, for a whole year, which documented in an extraordinarily humorous way the adventures of two recently married young Israelis during their travels in Europe. In that year, the column gained widespread popularity among readers and received many references within the "Letters to the Newspaper" section. The reason for this was not only the unique style of the author of the column, but also the fact that he refused—despite many hints he planted along the way—to identify himself, and signed under the pseudonym "A. Trempai." The readers' guesses ranged from Art Buchwald to Dan Ben-Amotz and Ephraim Kishon. Only after the couple finally returned to Israel, the author agreed to reveal his full name: Alex Carmel. Years later, Alex Carmel (1931–2002) became not only my father, but also a professor of history at the University of Haifa, who pioneered the research on the German Templers and the seven German colonies they built throughout Palestine at the end of the nineteenth century.

In July 1959, the couple sailed aboard the ship "Theodor Herzl" to Southern Europe, from there they continued by hitchhiking, and then in a car they bought, to Lapland, with the goal of reaching the Arctic Circle. The column below, which was published on August 14, 1959 and was titled "A Land Full of Swedes" describes the author's impressions of the northern country, which they visited on the way to their final destination.

> At this moment we park on the Arctic Circle, and if I only had a ladder to climb on, I would show you how to touch the North Star. In a little while,

after we have finished bathing and I have shaved my week-old beard, we are preparing to continue our way to the city of Jokkmokk, the capital of Swedish Upland. This metropolis, as we were told, is a huge settlement of 3,000 inhabitants, and if you take a good map, you can immediately prove that if Eilat [the most southern place of Israel - O.K.C] is the end of the world, then Jokkmokk is the beginning of the world. Anyway, it's 80 hours (you do the math of counting the days on your own, it doesn't get dark here at all and I'm already completely confused) since we last saw a human being in this desolate area, even though twenty or so hours ago, my wife broke out in the middle of the drive shouting "Here's a man", when we got closer we saw that it was just a fox standing on two legs leaning on a tree to observe a sitting squirrel and thinking what kind of a feast he would make if the squirrel cooperated with him and came down. Therefore, it should not be surprising that we are already curious to enter Jokkmokk and see again what normal people look like. All this is, of course, in case our car doesn't break down on the way. There are usually good roads in Sweden, but the roads in the north are now being repaired and the last section, of 1200 kilometers, was more like a camel's back than a road, not in regard to its colors but to the "humps". Apart from that, they drive on the left side here and in my first 20 kilometers in Sweden, until it became clear to me that this is probably a fairly accepted method, I did not have an easy time. At first I shouted at every driver who came in front of me "Idiot, we're not in England!", but then my wife explained to me that drunk driving is very common in this country and it's not worth getting excited because of some irresponsible drivers.

Only after a while, when "Trafik" stopped me, wrote me a traffic report and invited me to appear after three months at a court for traffic offenders in Stockholm, I began to understand that here it is probably quite customary to drive on the left side of the road.

I only hope that the judge, before whom I have to appear, will not take it too much to heart if he has to, on the appointed day, get along without me. To the traffic policeman's credit, I have to say that he would not have written the report if I had not, on this occasion of driving on the right side, been overtaking a car in a turn, at a speed of 100 kilometers per hour and in an urban area. Try to explain to him that I am traveling from Israel to Lapland and I don't have the time to play by the driving rules.

Sweden, as well known, is a monarchy and when someone breaks the law, it is immediately seen as an insult to the king. To you, the readers, I need not tell that I have nothing special against the King of Sweden. For my part, let him be healthy and strong, but even this won't convince me not to cross a white line when, at a distance of 500 kilometers in front of me and behind me, you can't see anything except a few squirrels or moose running on the road. However, the Swedish driver will in no way commit such an offense and when the road turns, for example, to the right (and if you deviate from it and continue straight you will roll into an abyss 200 meters deep) then he will definitely put his hand out and give you a sign that despite everything he is preparing to continue driving along the road and that he is not intending, at this point, to end his life by going down the abyss.

What else can be said about the Swedes that I didn't tell? Well, except for the ones who don't, they all have blonde hair, blue eyes and snub noses, they live in Swedish huts, eat Swedish plates, and even though "Ascot" tastes better... is better... [Israeli contemporary advertisement for cigarettes - O.K.C] they prefer Swedish cigarettes. They sell eggs by weight, their bread - either it is sweetened with sugar or it is spiced with licorice - and they only see the sun in the cinema. If it's not drizzling in Sweden, it's a clear sign that it's pouring rain. When we asked someone when summer is coming, he replied that he doesn't know exactly, but last year it was on Wednesday. Anyway, since we entered Sweden we haven't seen a single blue patch through the clouds and yesterday morning I saw that the mud formed in our car wheels had already started to grow mushrooms.

It is still difficult for me to judge the attitude of the Swedes towards the State of Israel. When we lingered one day in Stockholm, we encountered a group of people on the street who occasionally mentioned the name "Israel". Since some derogatory words were also said in connection with the subject, my wife decided that these people were members of the European Nazi organization headquartered in the Swedish city of Malmö. My wife is a Jew with loyal values and immediately pushed me to follow those people to discover the root of the evil. After following them for a long time, we finally arrived at a magnificent building where the World Jewish Congress was taking place at that time. It turns out that our informants were delegates to that congress. We have not met other anti-Semites in Sweden so far.

At this point, gentlemen, the mosquitoes, which swarm here by the millions, are getting on my nerves and I have to fold the typewriter, get in the car and continue driving. After all, we came here to visit Lapland and not to discuss Sweden's domestic policy. Those who are nevertheless interested in more details about this country should be patient until the editors of the Hebrew encyclopedia will finally reach the letter "S".

NOTES

1. *Dvar Hapoelet* 11, pp. 282–289.
2. Berl Balti, "Ben Gurion in Scandinavia", *Kol Ha'am*, August 31, 1962, p. 2.
3. ב"כשת לולאב ז"כ, הלשממה לש ב"כש/א"ס הבישי לכ-יטרפ, 26.9.62 Minutes of the government's 61 meeting ((ב"כש, 27 of Elul 5772, September 26, 1962.
4. Dan Laor, "Agnon's Life", Schocken Publishing House, Jerusalem and Tel Aviv, 1998, pp. 442–453.
5. *Things I Said in the Present of Invited Audience at the Home of the Israeli Envoy to the Scandinavian countries* (Stockholm, Beginning of Tammuz 1951),"From Myself to Myself", Schocken Publishing House, Jerusalem and Tel Aviv, 1976, pp. 41–42.
6. *Life of Agnon*, Dan Laor, Schocken Publishing House, Jerusalem and Tel Aviv, 1998, p. 447.
7. Ibid.
8. Ibid., p. 453.

Index

A
Addis Ababa, 96
Adult education, 70
Afro-Asian Institute, 41
Agnon, Esther, 123
Agnon, Shmuel Yosef, 115
Aid policy, 37
Almogi, Yosef, 33
Alterman, Nathan, 25
Amidar, 53
Amos, Yahil, 116
Arab pressure, 107
Arctic Circle, 126
Aroch, Arie, 40
Asher, Gad, 59
Assaf, Simcha, 76
Avnon, Zvi, 40

B
Ballad of the Swedish Hut, The, 63
Bandung conference, 30
Barkat, Reuven, 36
Beit Berl College, 84

Beit-Hamidrash Le-morei am (School for Educators of the People), 70
Ben-Amotz, Dan, 126
Ben Gurion, David, 30
Ben-Zvi, Mina, 94
Bergman, Hugo, 74
Bernadotte, Folke, 32
Best, Werner, 18
Bet Ha'Emek, 63
Brandt, Willy, 46
Brody, Avraham, 125
Buber, Martin, 69
Buchwald, Art, 126
Burg, Yosef, 7, 61

C
Carmel, Alex, 115
Carmiel, Moshe, 96
Casablanca Declaration, 101
Center for Jewish Adult Education (Mittelstelle für jüdische Erwachsenbildung), 73
Childs, Marquis, 4
Cohen, Idov, 61

Cold War, 3, 31
Community development, 91
Cooperative Movement, 96
Council for the Promotion of Israeli Heritage, 61
Council of the Socialist International, 37

D
Damari, Shoshana, 11
Davar, 25
"Denmark Square", 23, 25
  in Hof HaCarmel in Haifa, 25
  in Jerusalem, 25
Developing countries, 37
Development aid, 43
Dialogic principle in education, 77
Dinur, Ben Zion, 74
Dror Israel Movement, 84
Dvar Hapoelet (journal), 116

E
Eban, Abba, 30
Eichmann trial, 19
Eilat, 127
Erlander, Tage, 42
Eshkol, Levi, 55
Esther, 123
European Union, 33

F
Feibel, Berthold, 71
Fleeman, Moshe, 96
Folk high school, 76
Food and Agriculture Organization (FAO), 92
Freudenberg, Gideon and Hadassah, 74

G
Gerhardsen, Einar, 42
Gerstensang, Dov, 20
Gillon, Carmi, 26
Goldberg, Leah, 12
Government 1962:100 Bill, 93
Grundtvig, N.F.S., 23, 70

H
Haaretz (newspaper), 19
Hadassah Hospital, 41
Haifa, 37
Hammarskjöld, Dag, 34
Hamsun, Knut, 11
Hebrew University of Jerusalem, 72
Hechalutz, 20
Herut (newspaper), 11
Histadrut (Israel's General Federation of Labor), 34
Hultafors, 126

I
International Agricultural Development Cooperation, 41
International Council of Social Democratic Women, 92, 95
International Labour Organization (ILO), 103
International Organization of Consumers Unions, 92
Israeli-Arab/Palestinian conflict, 2
Israeli nuclear program, 2
Israel Scandinavian Maritime Agency, 57
Israel's Labor Movement, 35

J
Jacob A. Lewison Company, 60
Jewish Agency, 53
Jokkmokk, 127

INDEX 133

K
Kalman, Yaron, 71
Kampmann, Viggo, 39
Katzenelson, Shulamit, 84
Kfar Ahim, 58
Kfar Masaryk, 102
Khoushy, Abba, 104
Kibbutz Barkai, 62
King Christian X, 18
Kishon, Ephraim, 126
Kold, Christen, 78
Kol Ha'am (newspaper), 119
Kreisky, Bruno, 46
Kuper, Yehuda, 20

L
Lagerkvist, Pär, 126
Lange, Halvard, 42
Lapland, 126
Lassen, Gilbert, 25
Lehi, 32
Leibovitch, Yehoshua, 74
Leo (Yehuda Pinchas) Cohen, 30
Lie, Haakon, 34
Lillehammer, 125
Lindgren, Astrid, 11
Living word, 77
Locker, Berl, 75

M
Maariv (newspaper), 59
Mapai (Israeli Social Democratic party), 27
MASHAV, 39
Meir, Golda, 33
Melchior, David Werner, 19
Michanek, Ernst, 100
Moe, Finn, 36
Molad (journal), 83
Mount Carmel Training Center, 41

N
Nahariya, 59
Nasser, Gamal Abdel, 31
Nativ, 95
NATO, 2
Negev, 52
Neutral bloc, 37
NIB, 97
Nissan, Avraham, 123
Nkrumah, Kwame, 101
Nobel Prize, 123
Non-Aligned States Organization, 30
NORDEK, 33
Nordic Council, 4, 32
Nordic Council of Ministers, 5, 32
Nordic Labor Agreement, 5
Nordic model, 109
Nordic Security Pact, 33
Norrköping, 11
Norwegian Labor Party, 34
Norwegian Union of Seafarers, 34

O
Odense, 11
Organization for Economic Cooperation and Development (OECD), 5

P
Palme, Olof, 43
Periphery doctrine, 31
Petah Tikva, 11
Poriya, 59
Puutalo Oy (company), 60

R
Reiser, Jaakov, 53
Remez, Aharon, 96
Righteous among the Nations, 20
Rivkin-Brick, Anna, 11
Rottenstreich, Nathan, 74

Rudling, Anna, 100
Ryslinge, 79

S
Sandström, Emil, 32
Sapir, Pinchas, 42
Scandinavian Seamen's Church, 11
Schick, Konrad, 11
Schleswig-Holstein, 81
Sde Boker, 52
Segev, Tom, 26
Seidenfaden, Gunnar, 44
Shazar, Zalman, 75
Sheba, Chaim, 59
Sheerit hapleta, 52
Shenhabi, Mordechai, 19
Sholem, Gershom, 74
Simon, Ernst, 74
Singer, Isaac Bashevis, 11
Slor, Benjamin, 19
Social Democratic Women's Federation, 96
Social Development Division of the UN, 95
Södermanland, 108
Solel Bone (company), 53
Soroptimist International, 95
Stockholms Tidningen (newspaper), 93
Suez Canal, 33
Suez war, 13
Swedish-Haifa Committee, 96
Swedish International Development Authority (SIDA), 40
Swedish-Israel Aid, 58
Swedish Language, The (poem), 25
Swedish Social Democratic Women's Federation, 95
Swedish Theological Institute, 11
Swedish Union of Seafarers, 35
Swedish Workers' Union, 35

T
Taanach, 102
Tabor House, 11
Talbiyeh, 70
Third Way, 4
Thorsson, Inga, 94
Tiedje, Johannes, 81
Trade Union Confederation, 96
Transit camps ("Maabarot"), 57
Trondheim, 11
Tzrifin, 59

U
Ulpan Akiva, 84
UN, 31, 91
UN Commission on the Status of Women, 95
Union of Danish Seafarers, 35
Union of Finnish Seafarers, 34
United Arab Republic, 43
United Nations Children's Fund (UNICEF), 92
United Nations Development Programme (UNDP), 107
United Nations Educational, Scientific and Cultural Organization (UNESCO), 41, 91
United Nations Special Committee on Palestine (UNSCOP), 32
U Nu, 38

V
Volcani Center for Agricultural Research, 41

W
Waffen SS, 27
Wallenberg, Raoul, 8
War of 1967, 106
War of 1973, 106

Weizmann, Chaim, 71
Weizmann Institute of Science, 41
Weizmann, Vera, 59
Welfare state, 4
Widhe, Etti, 96
Women's Corps of the Israel Defense Forces, 95

Y

Yad Vashem (institution), 19
Yahil, Chaim, 36
Yahil, Leni, 21
Yanuv, 58
Yishuv, 8

Printed in the USA
CPSIA information can be obtained
at www.ICGtesting.com
JSHW011750091224
75095JS00004B/55